MELANIN, MAY I ?

coloring for the culture™

CONCEPT AND ILLUSTRATIONS BY

JASMINE STRICKLAND

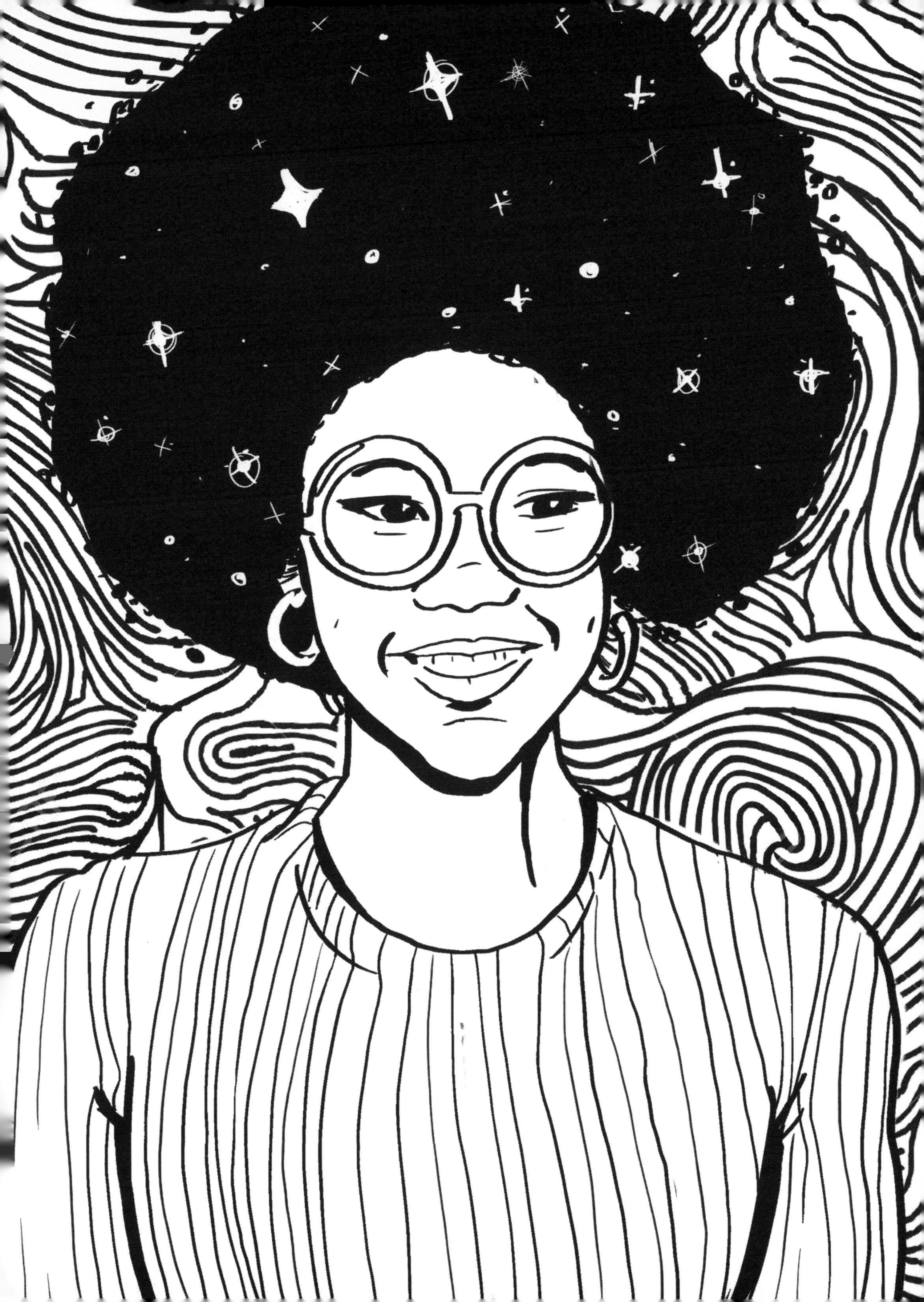

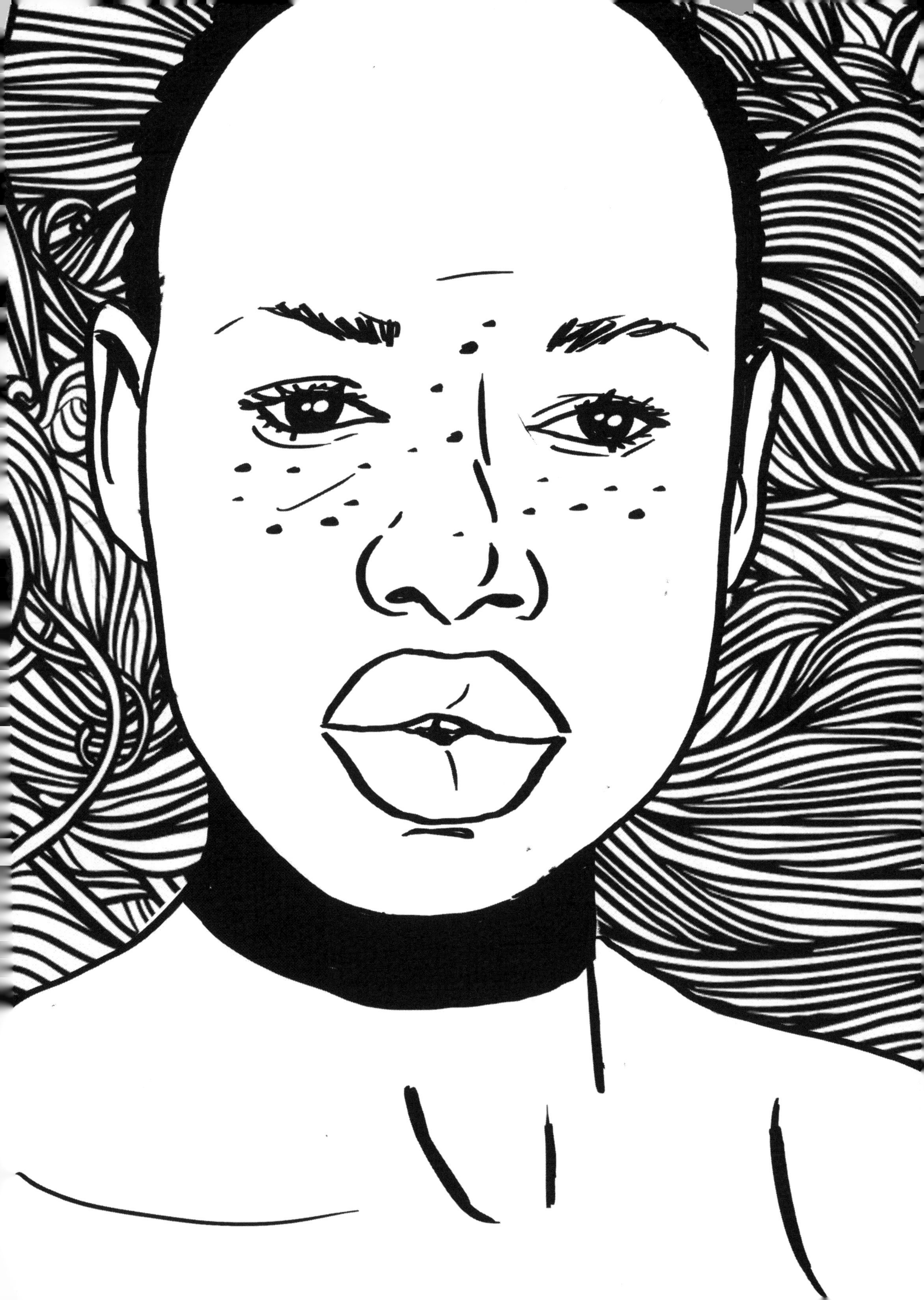

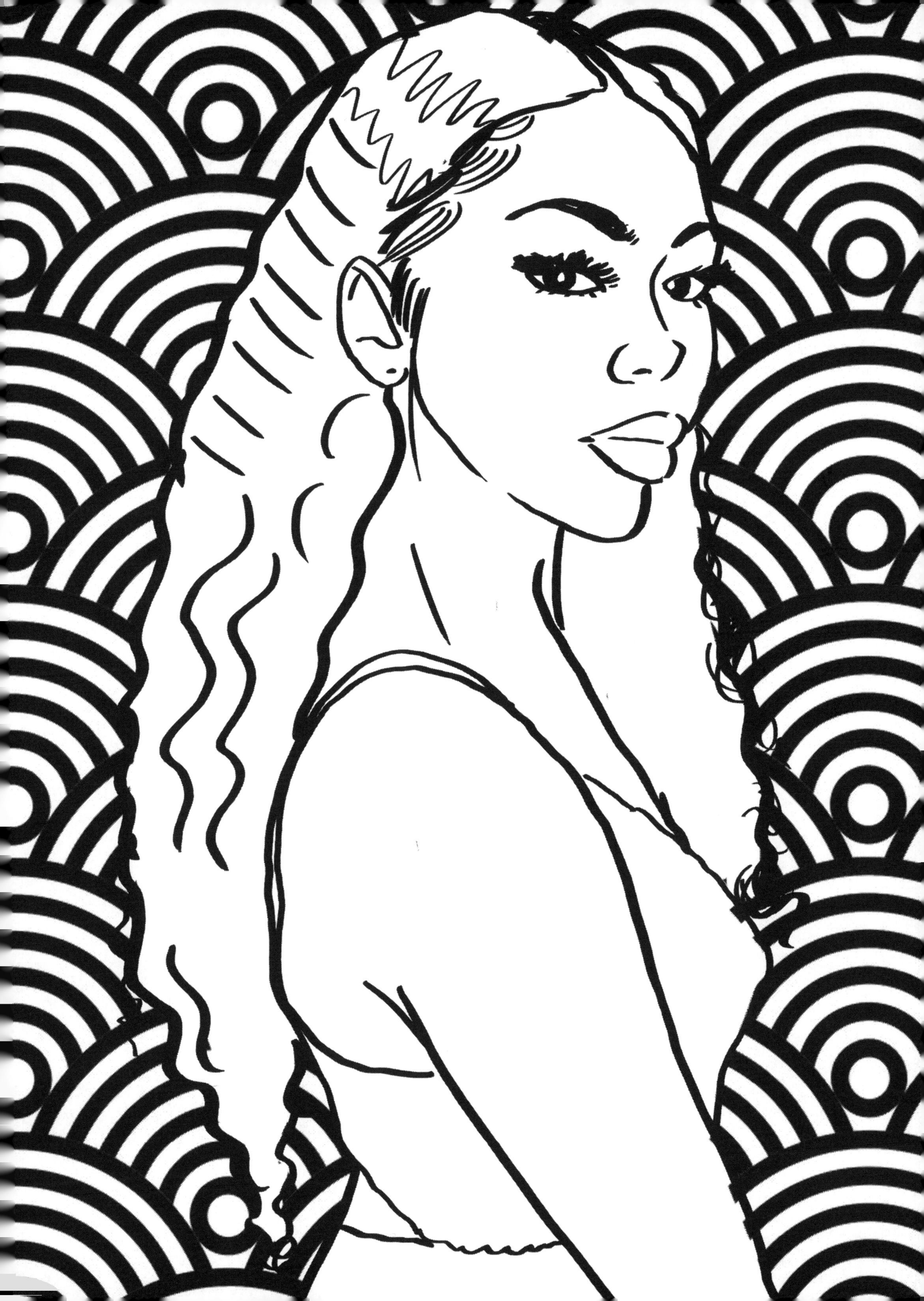

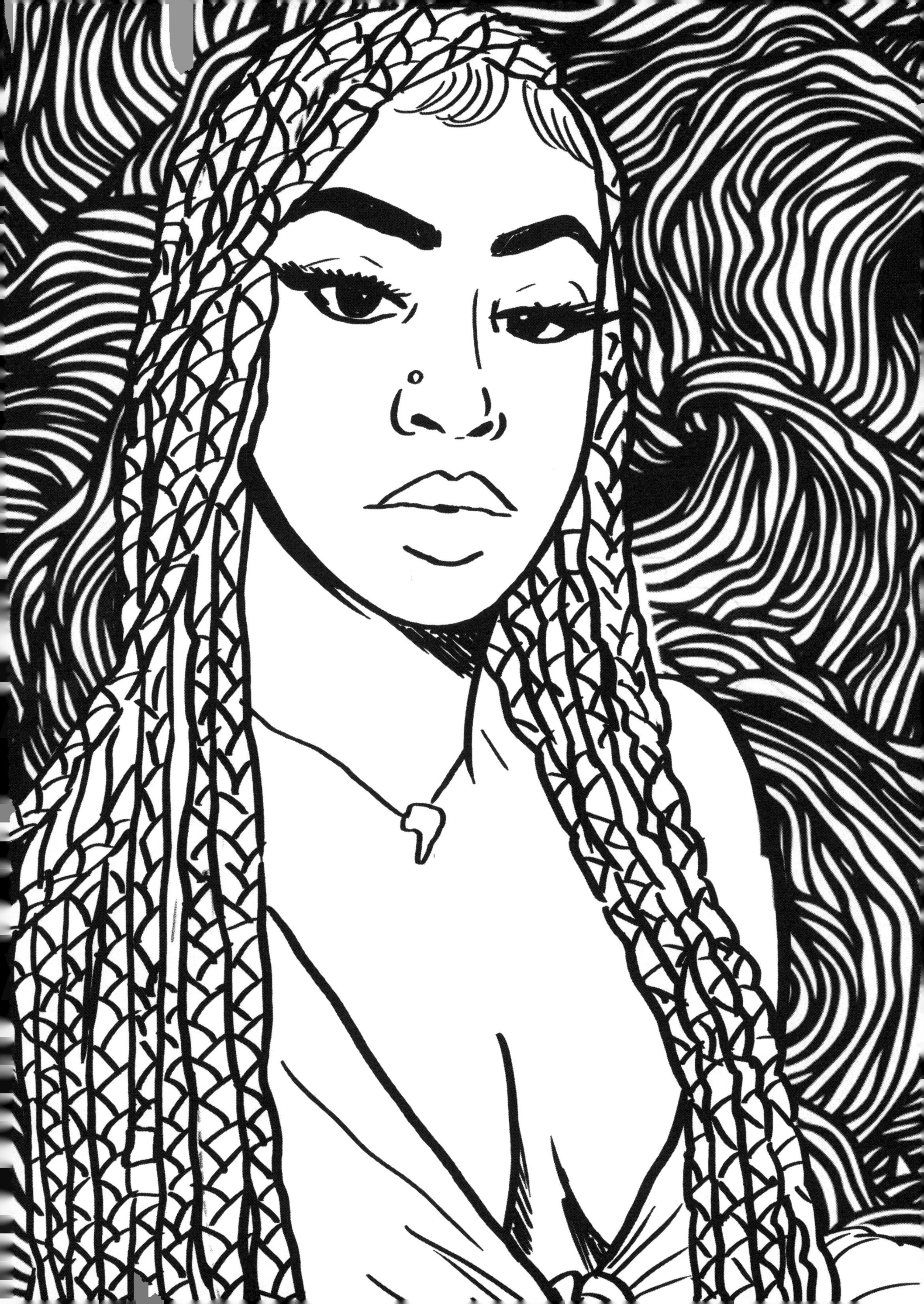

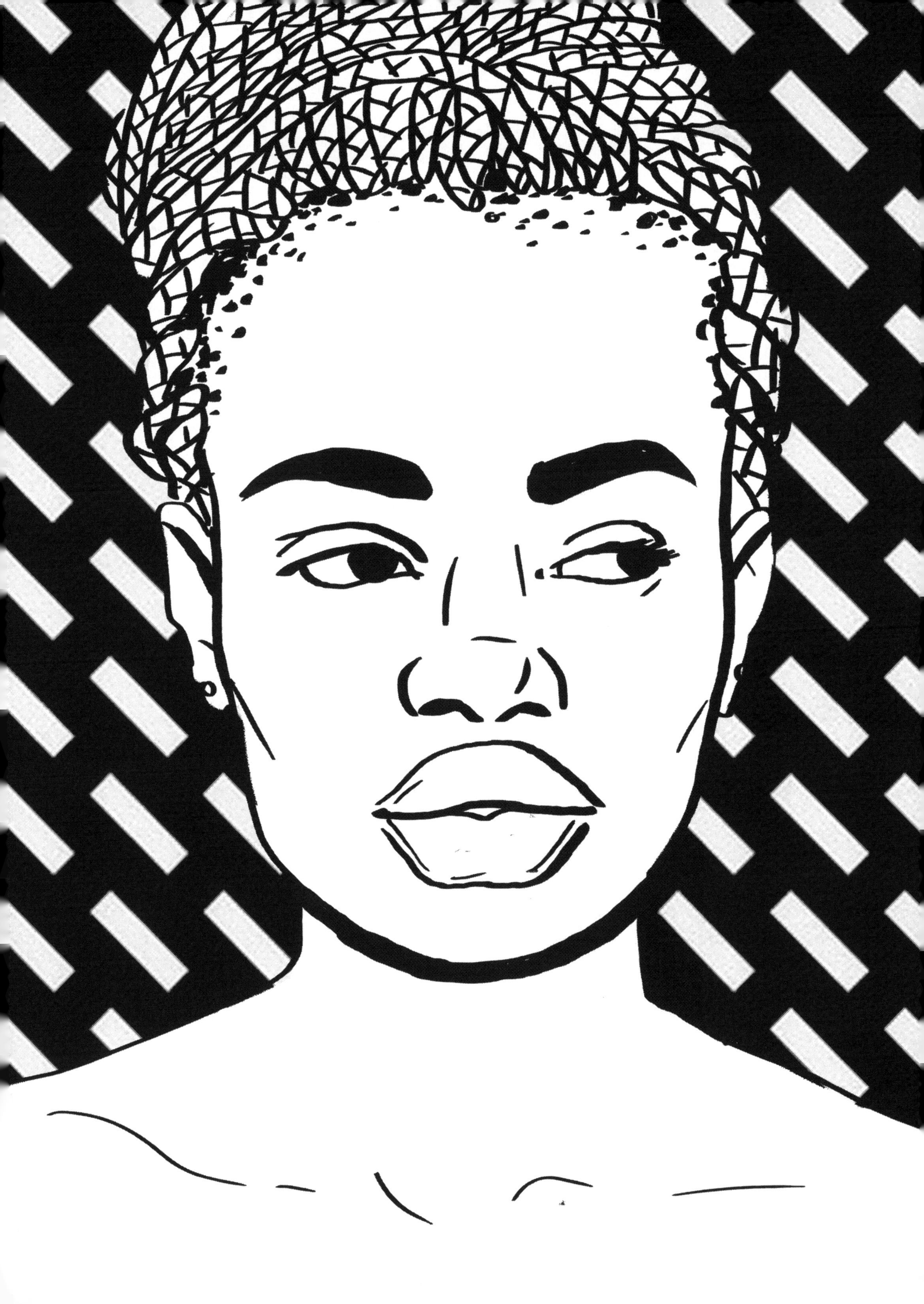

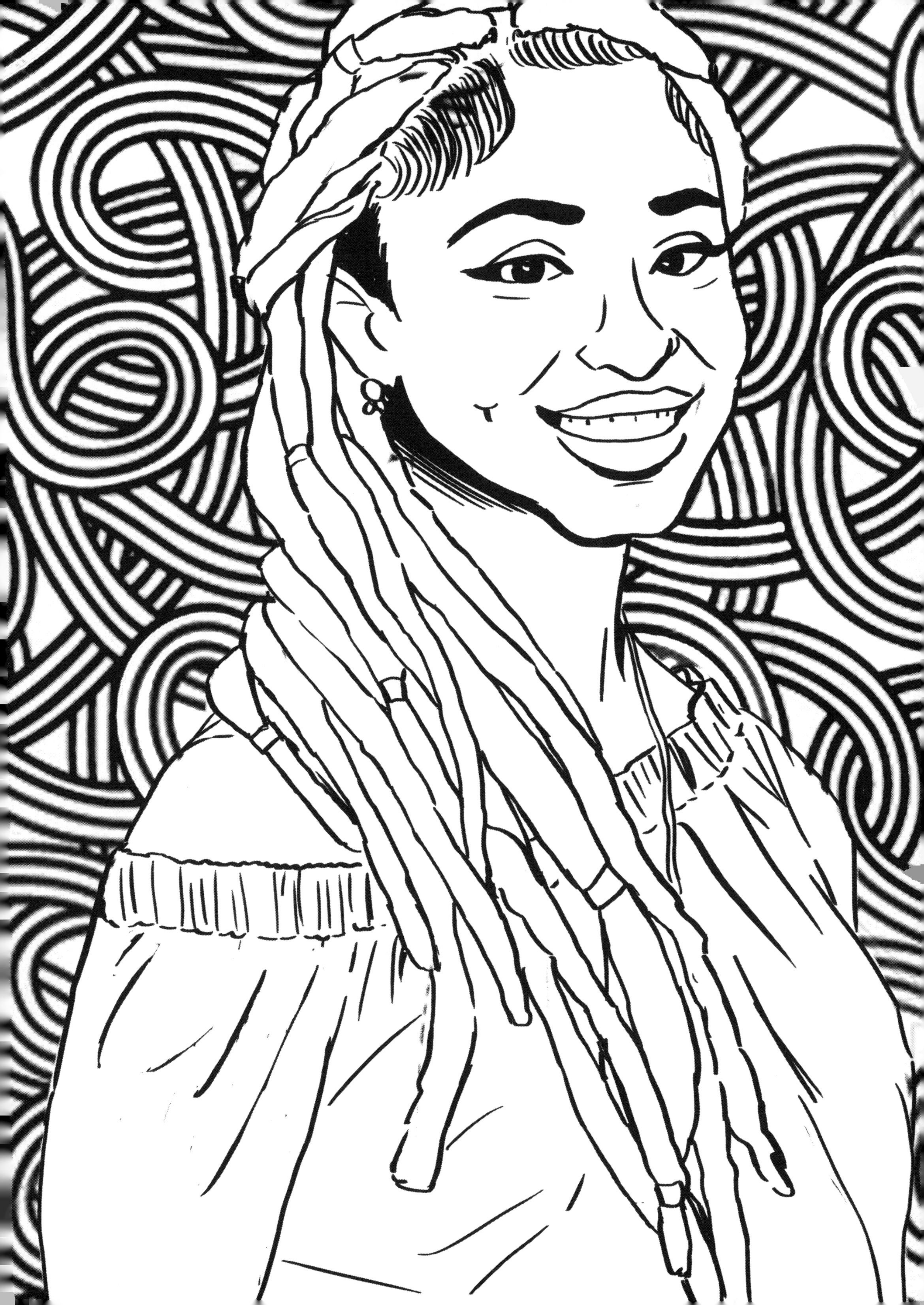

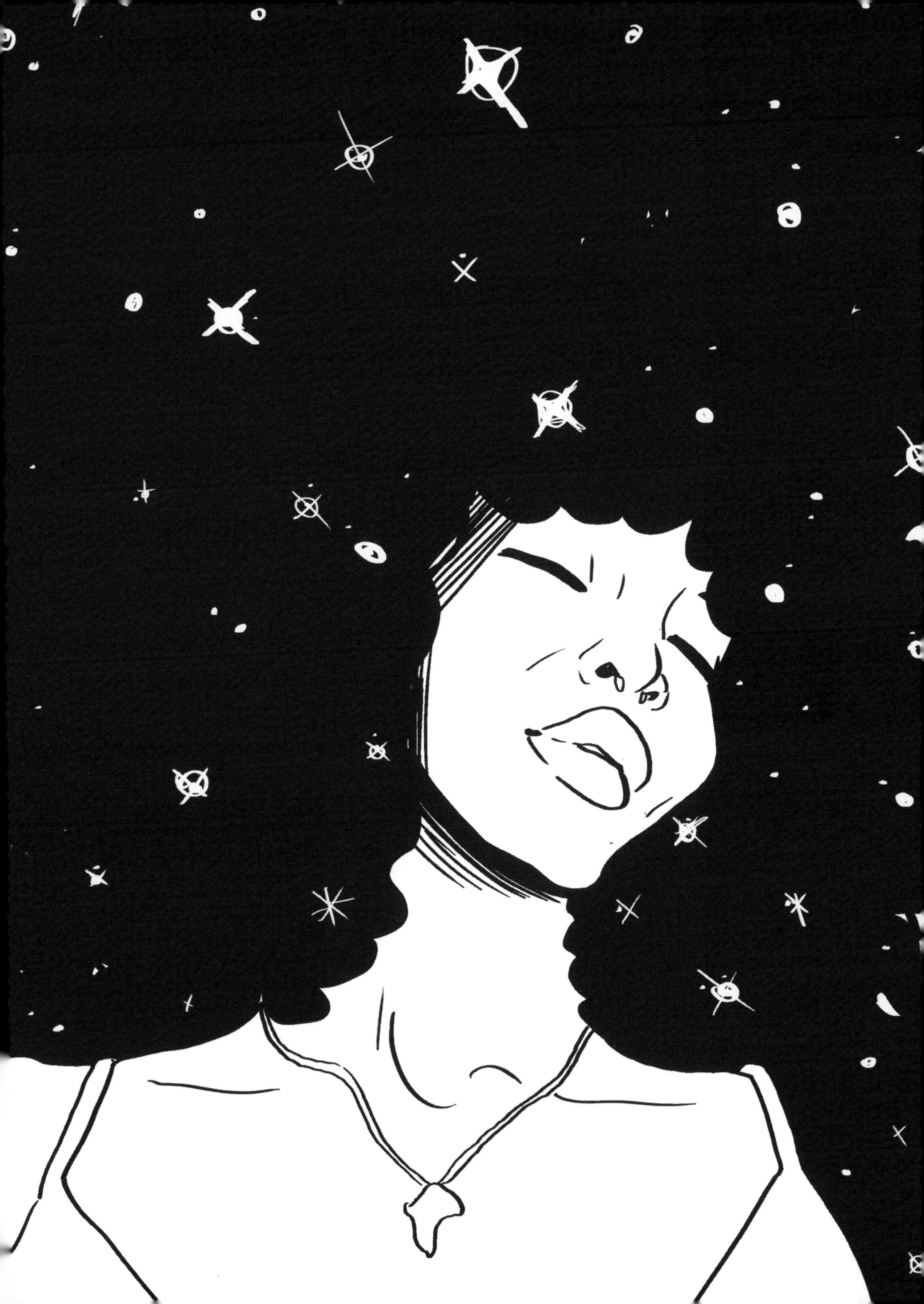

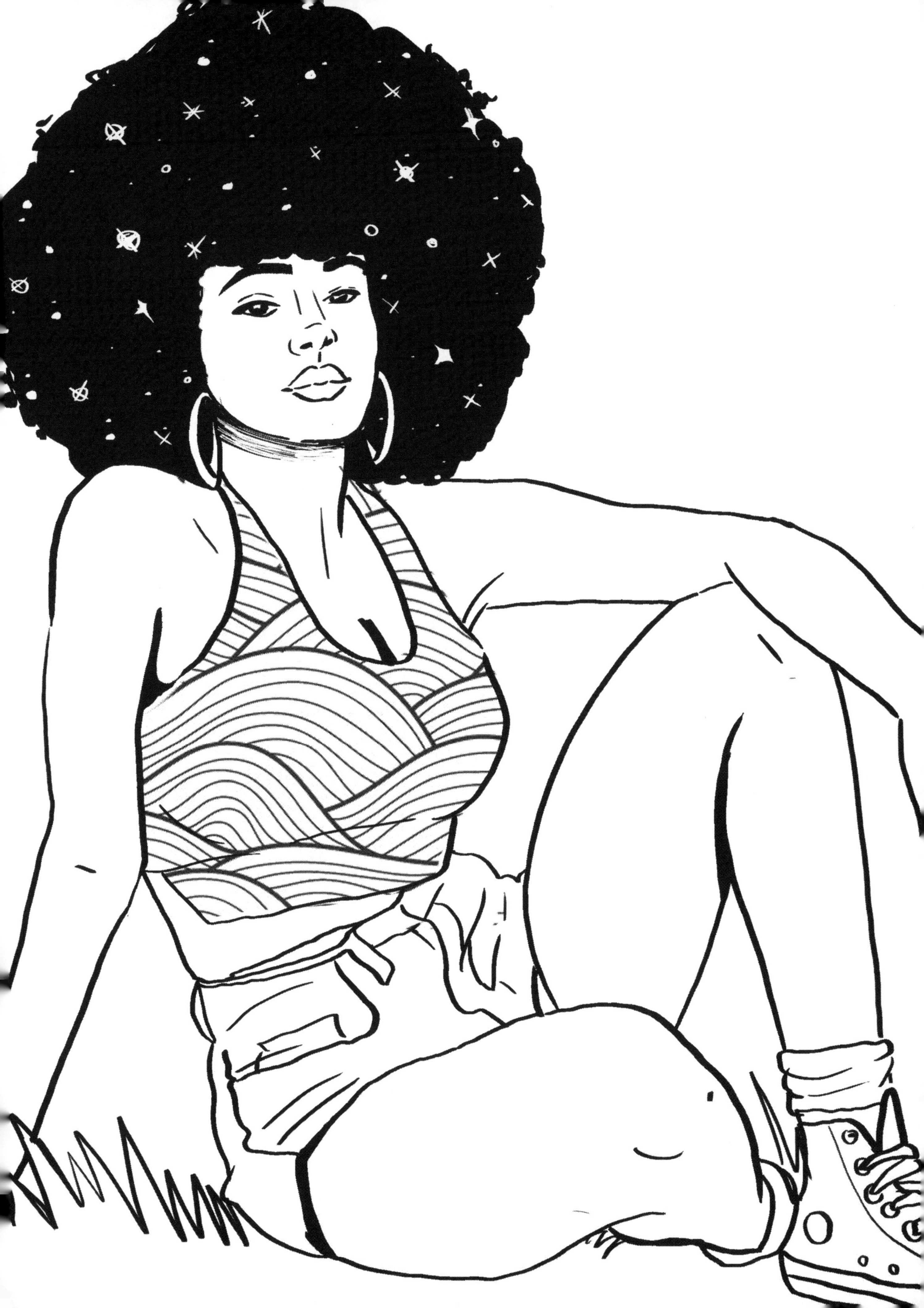

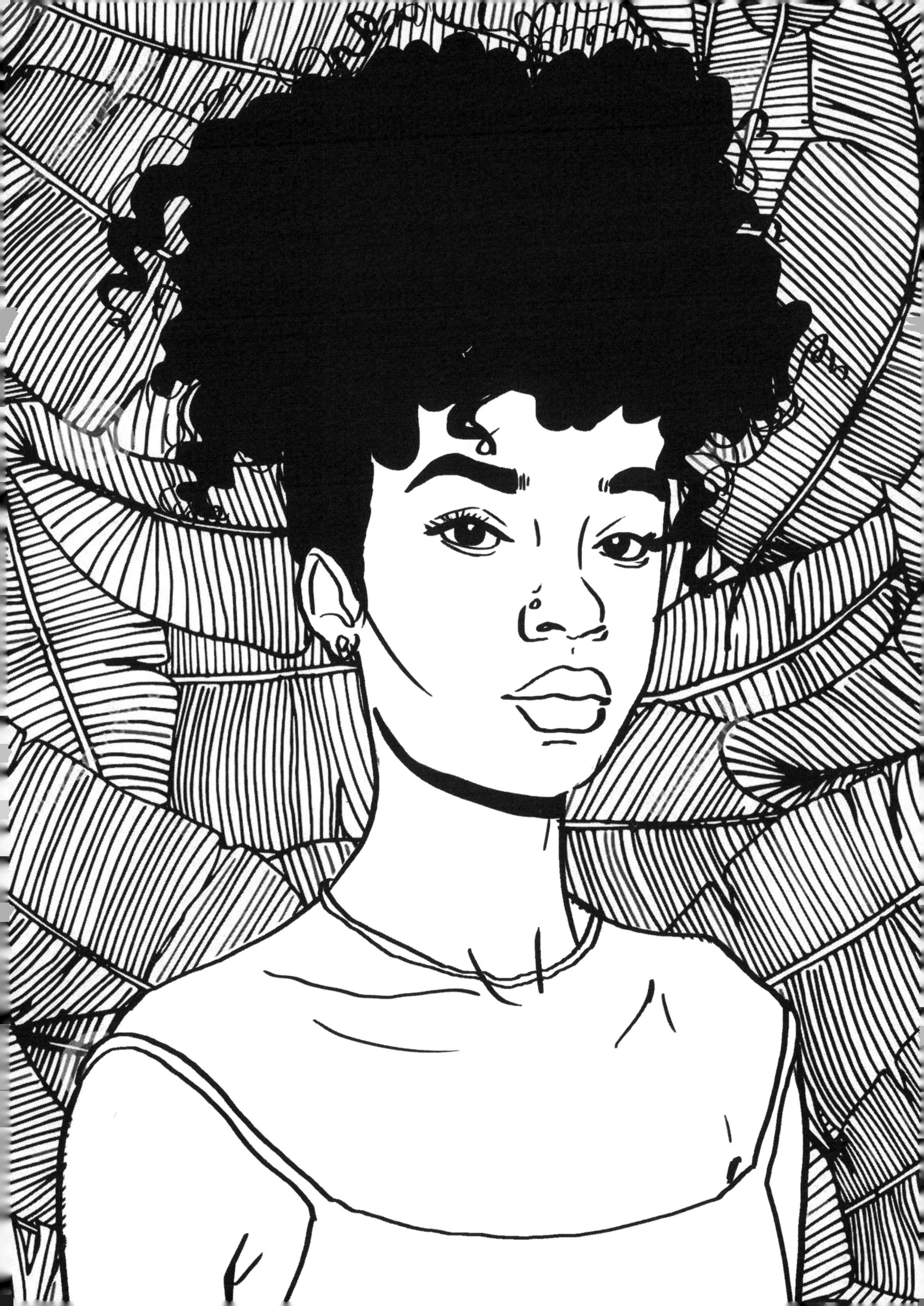

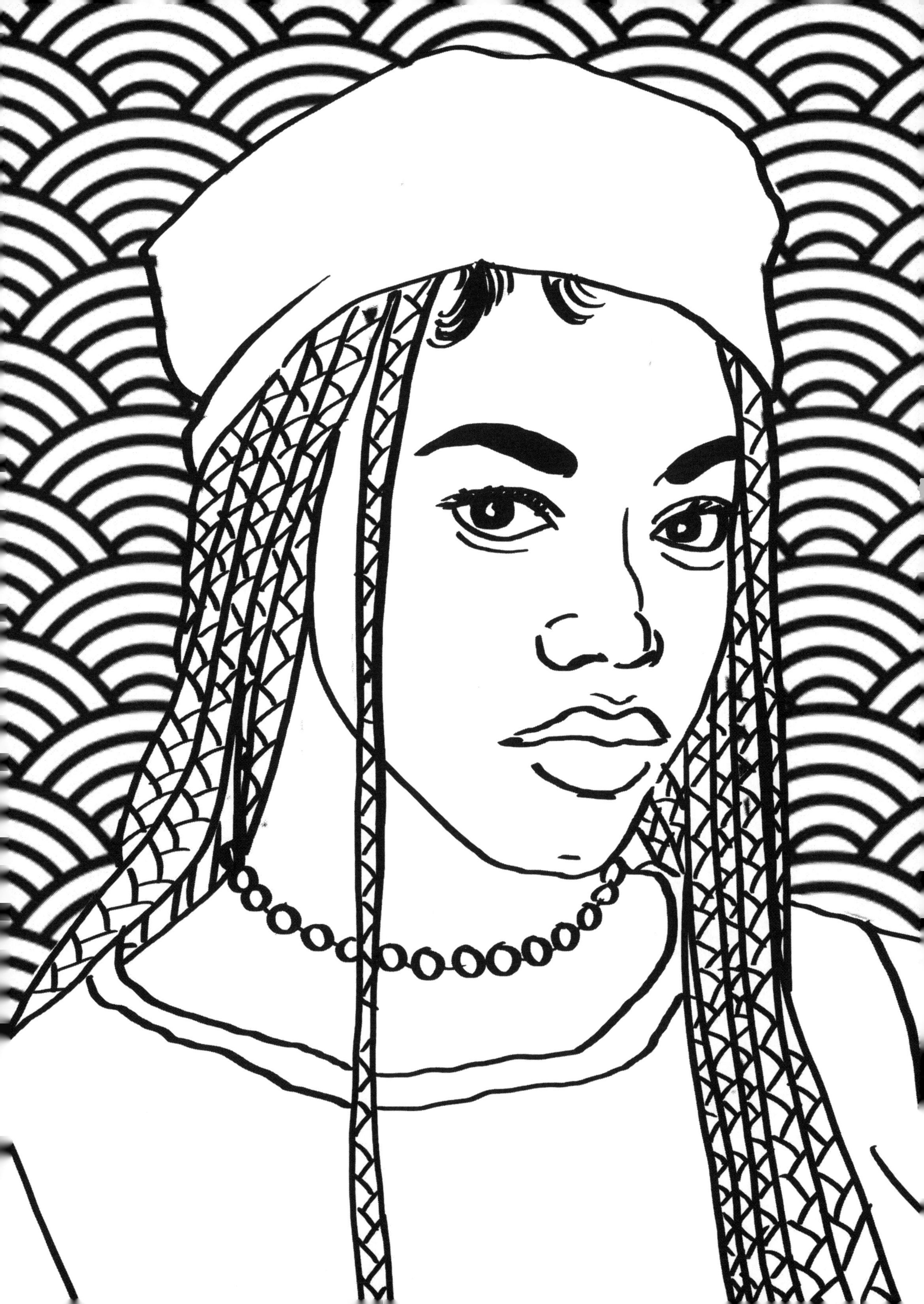

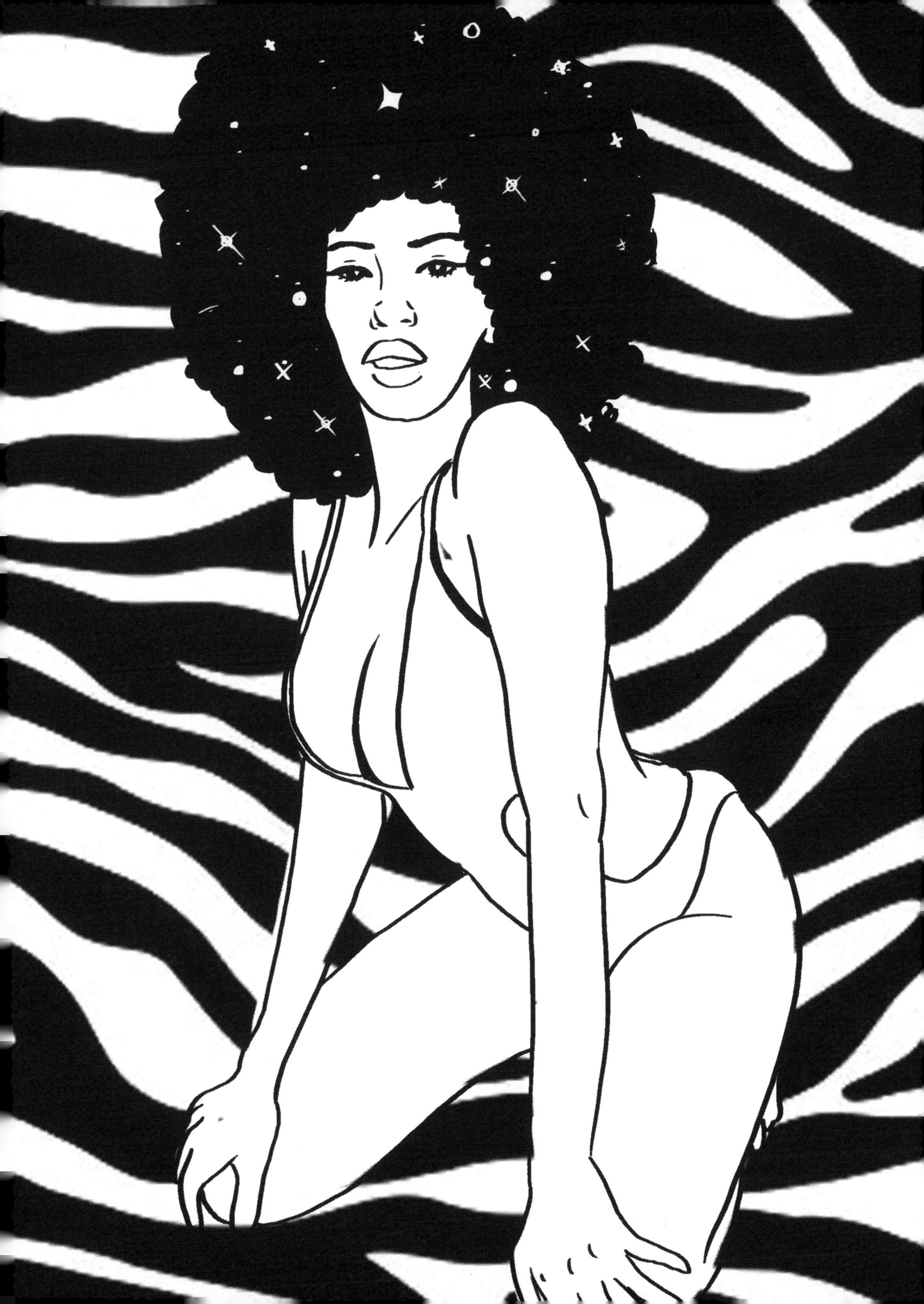

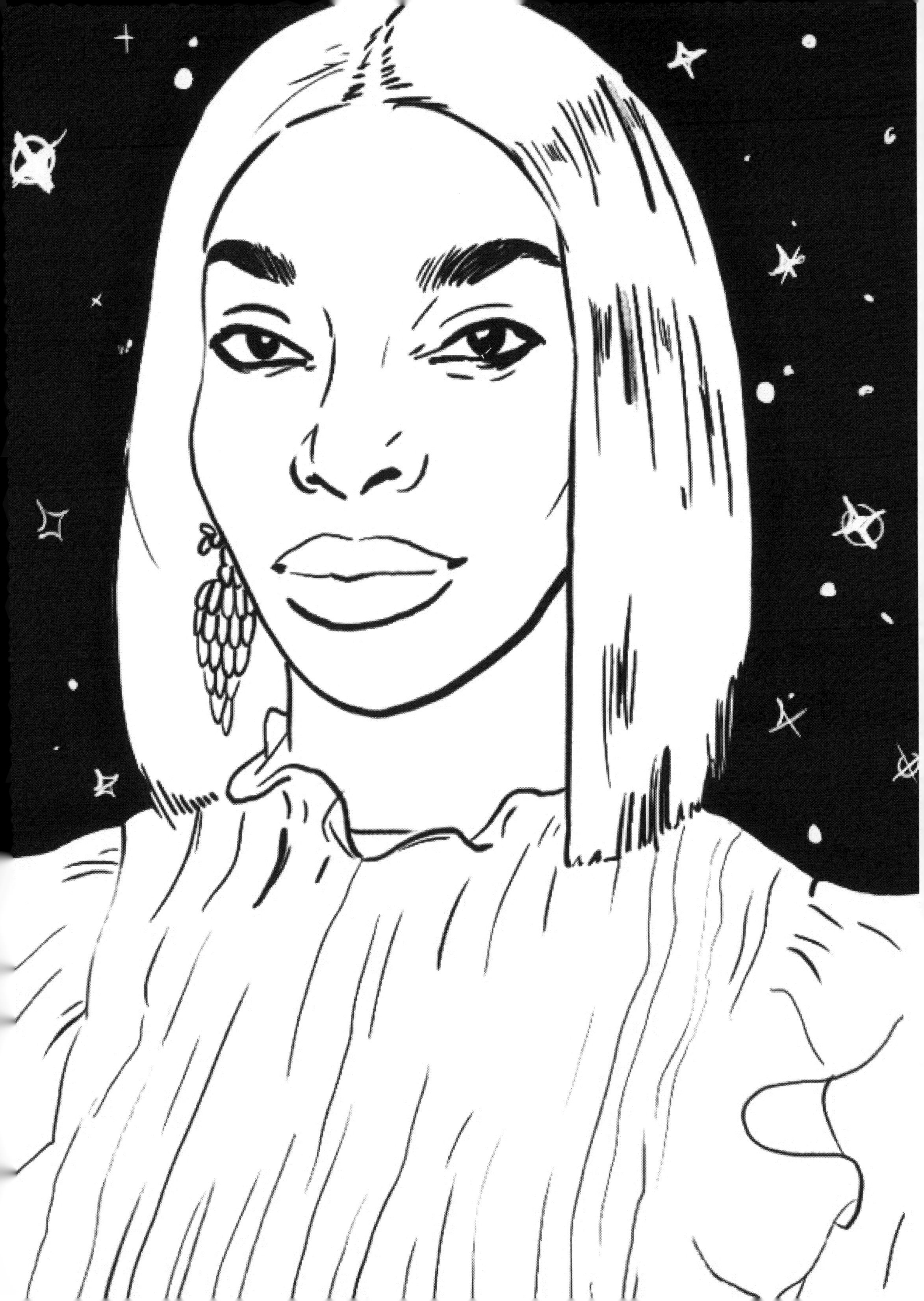

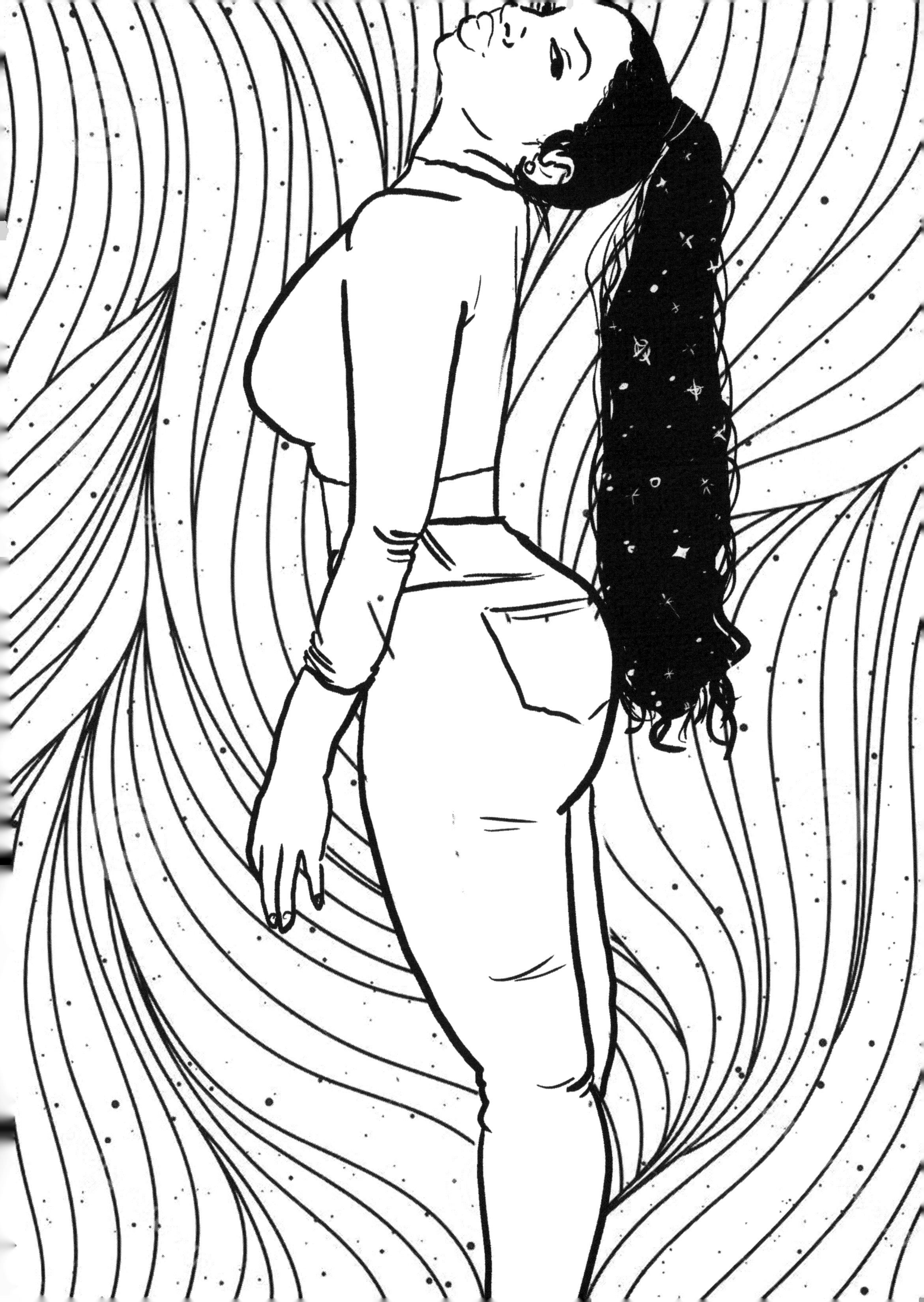

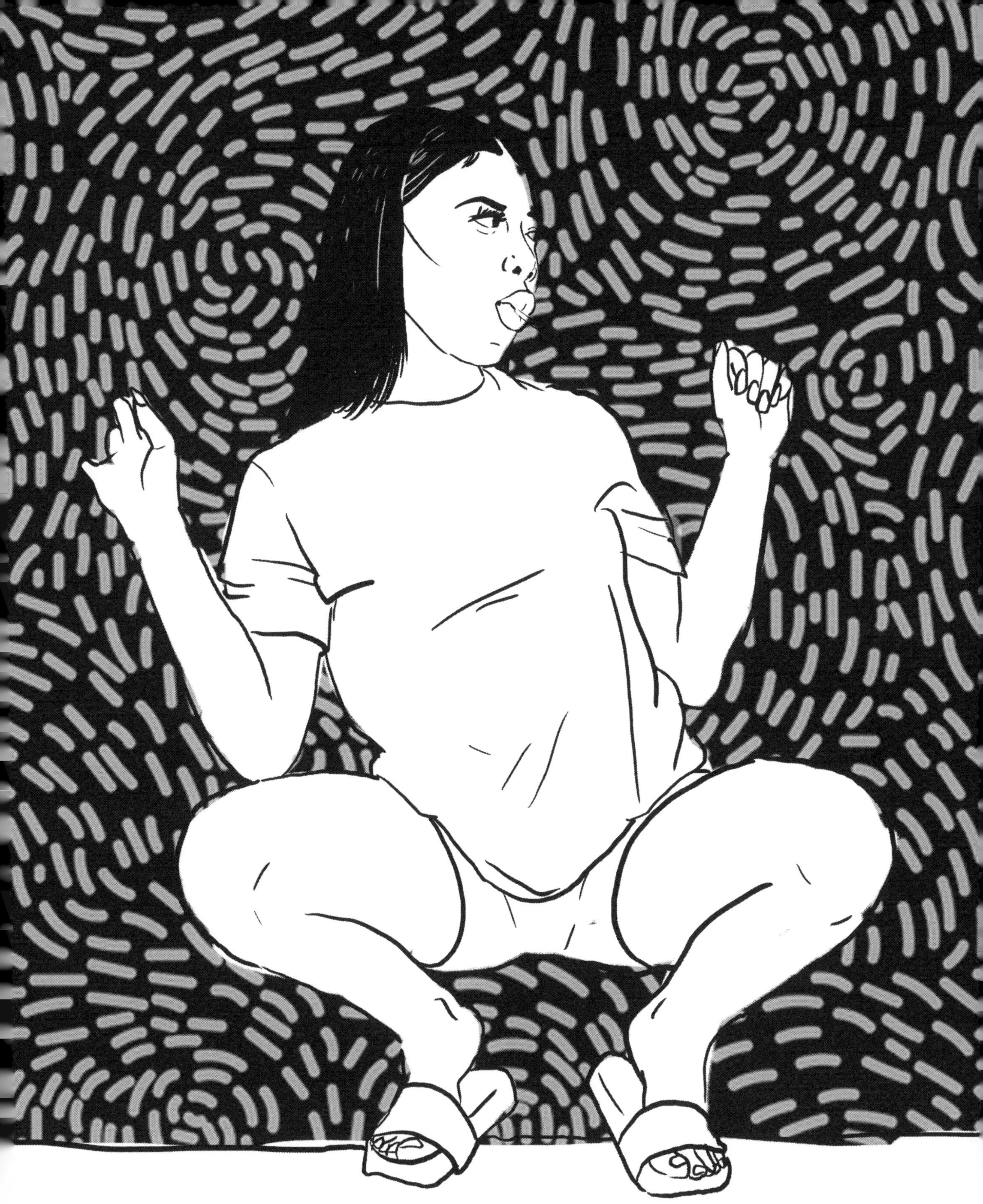

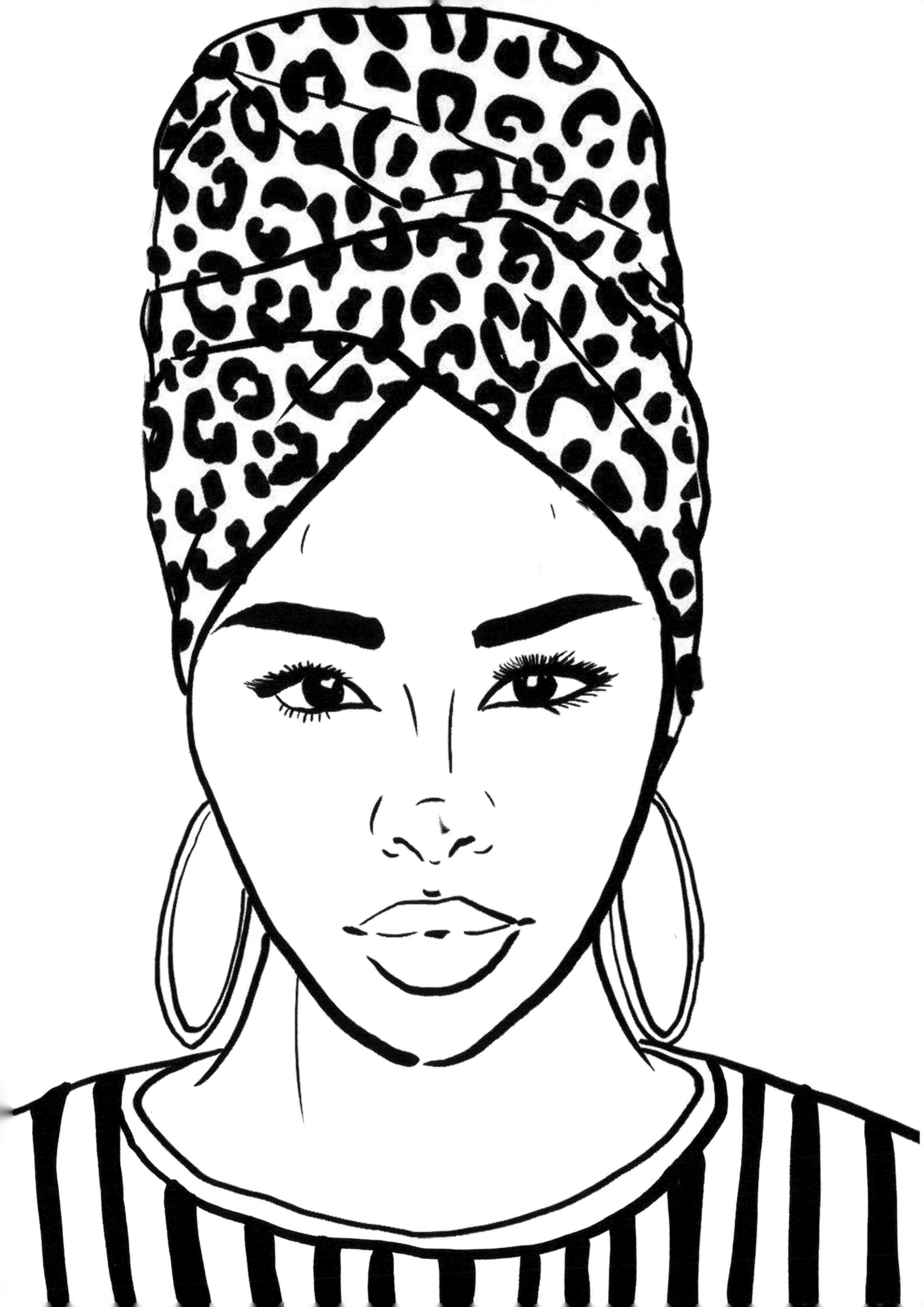

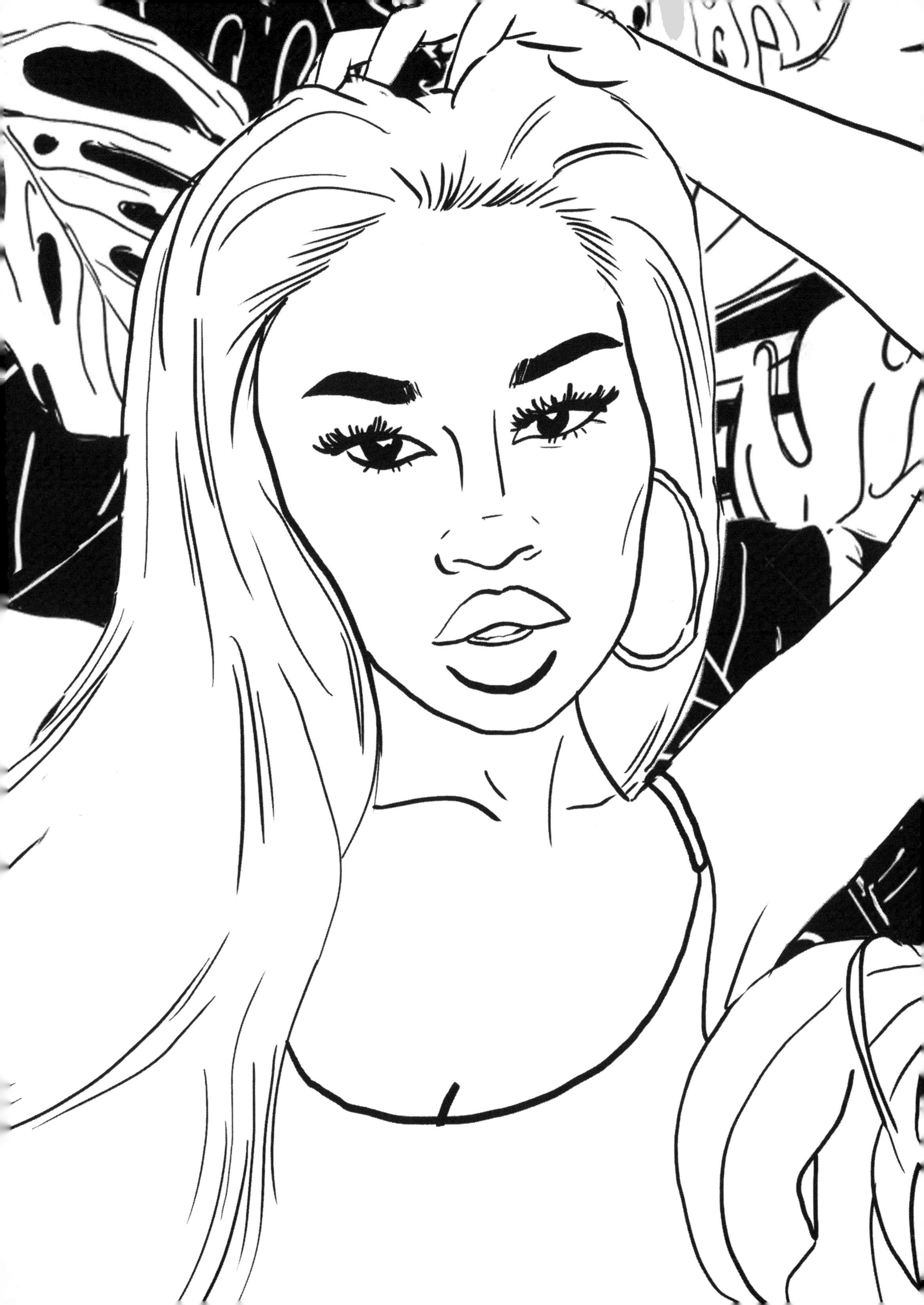

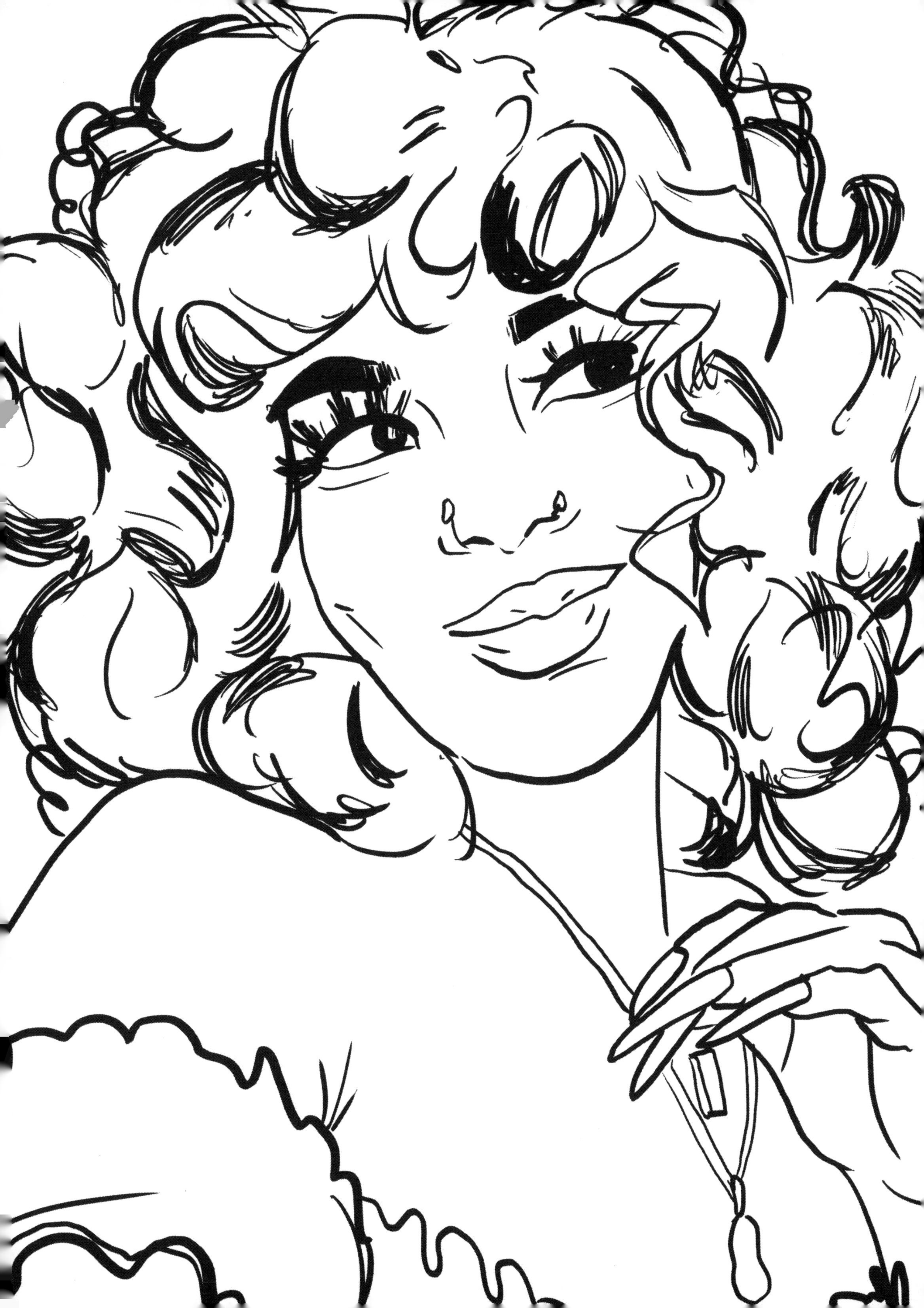

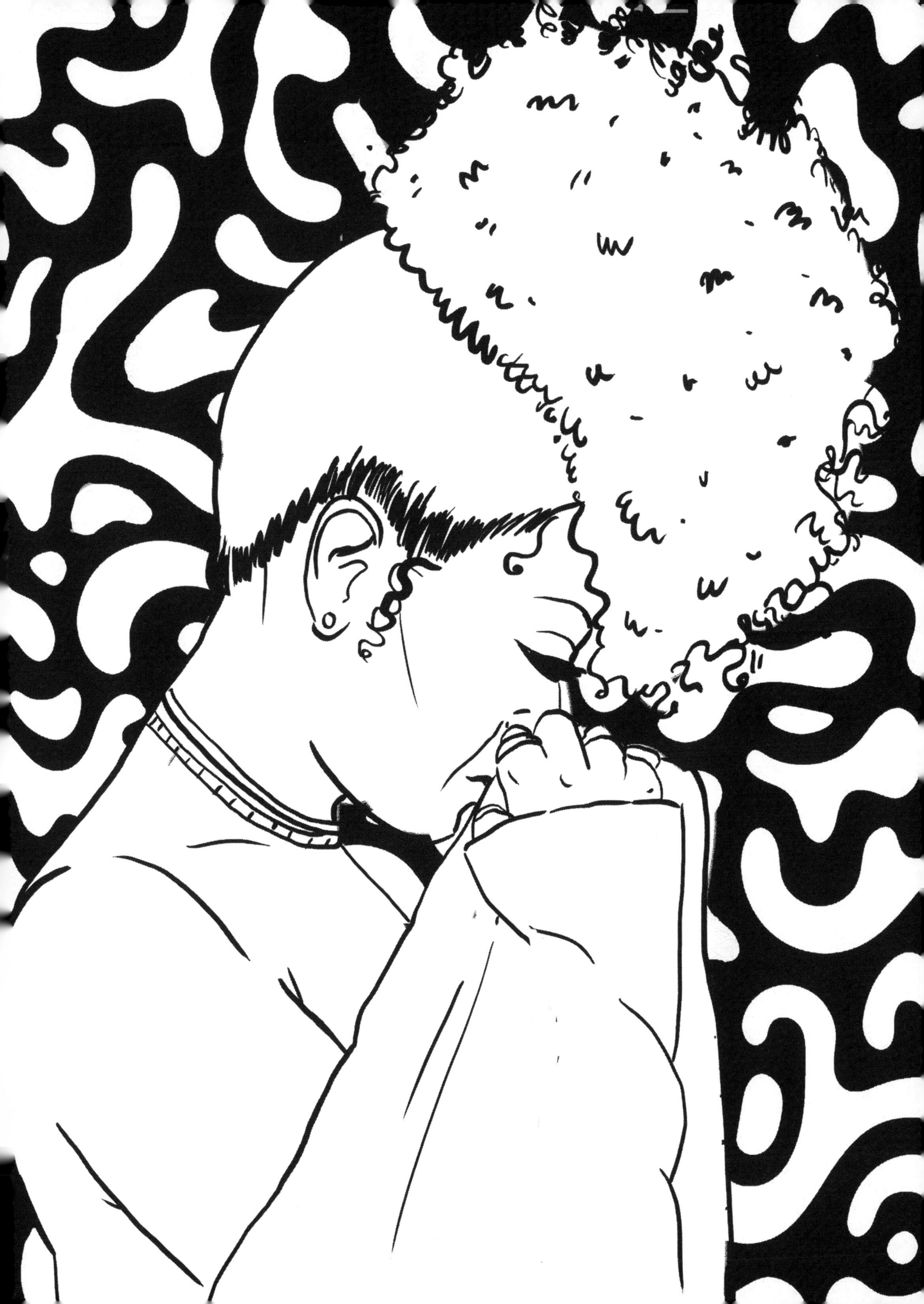

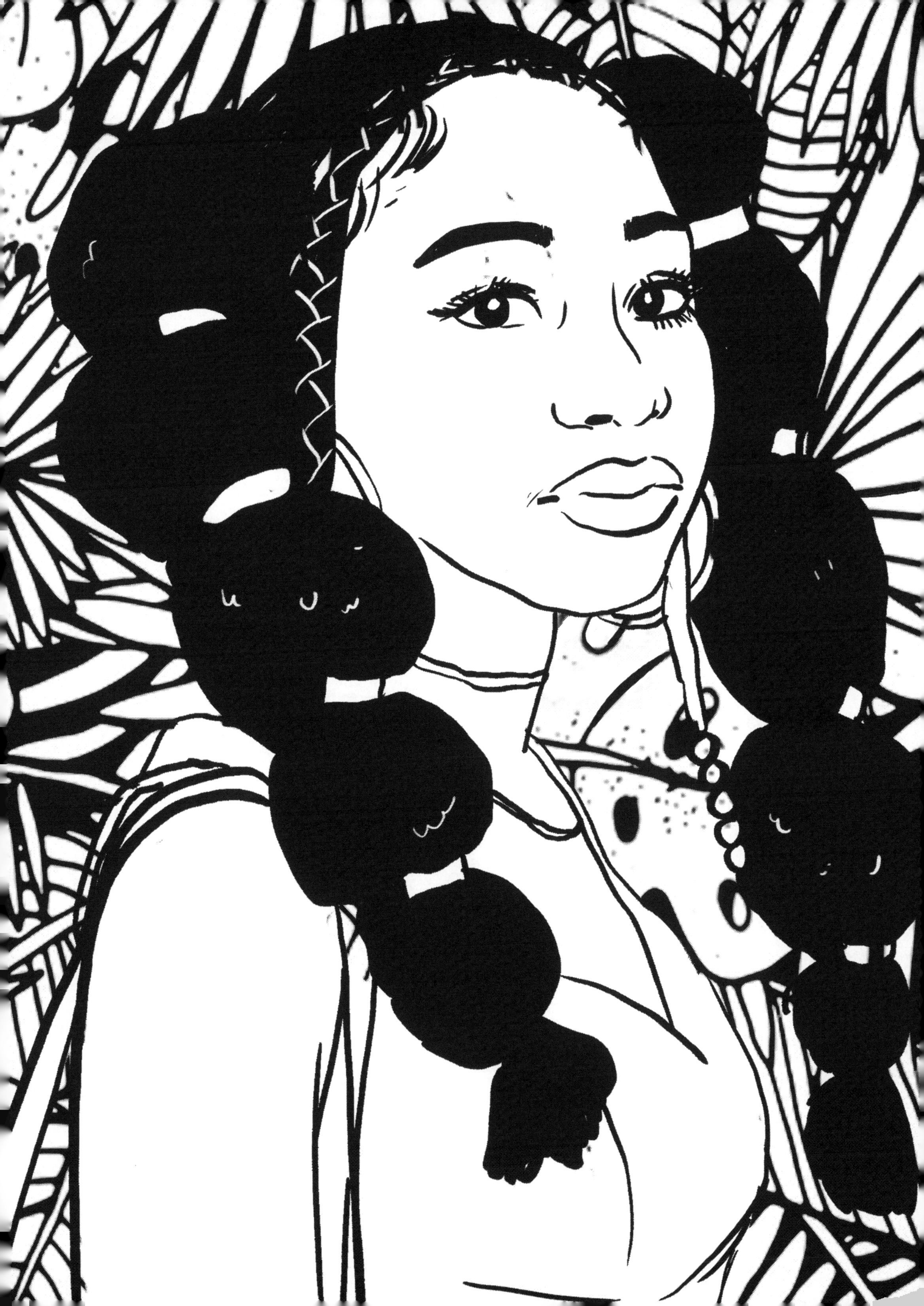

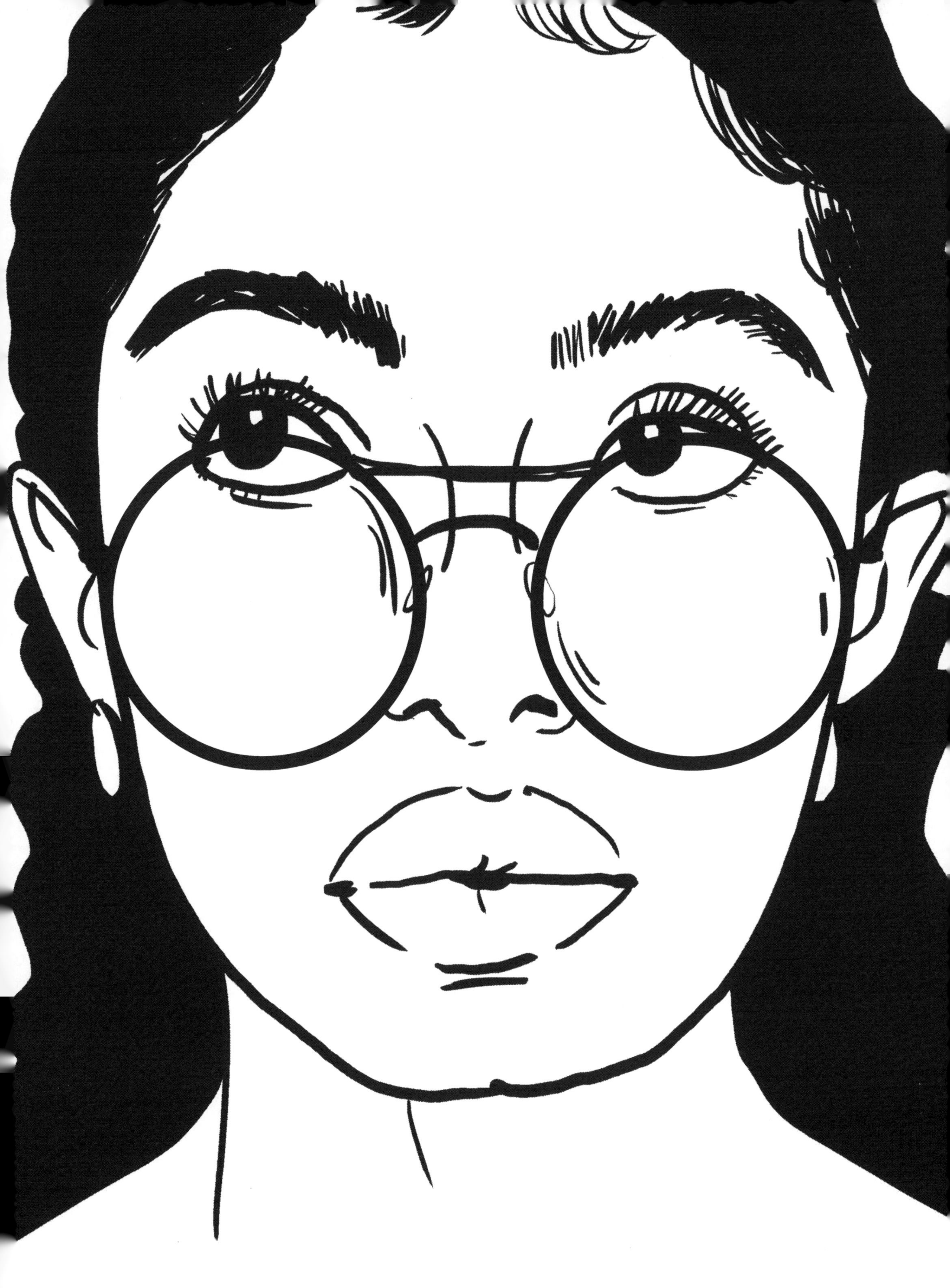

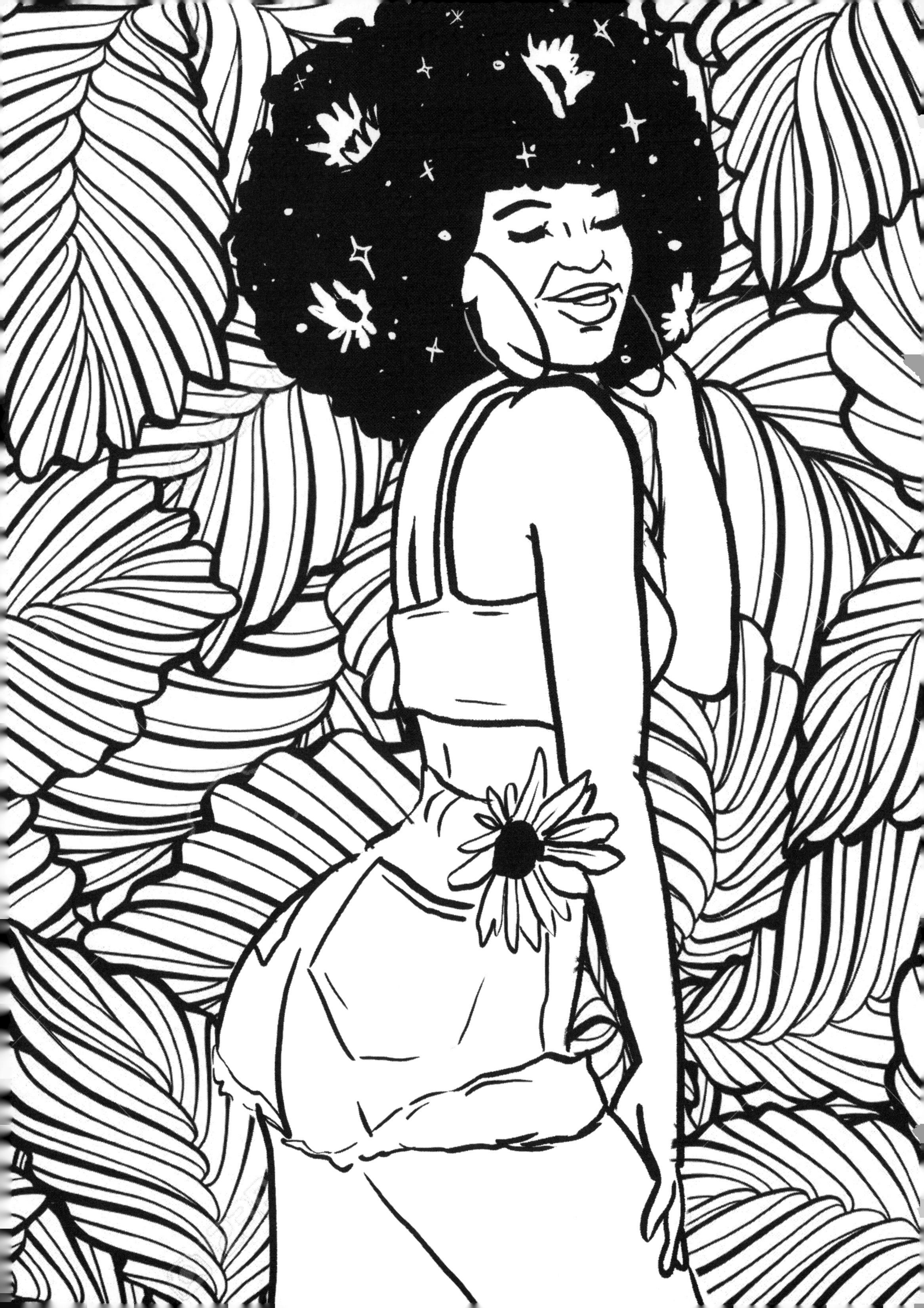

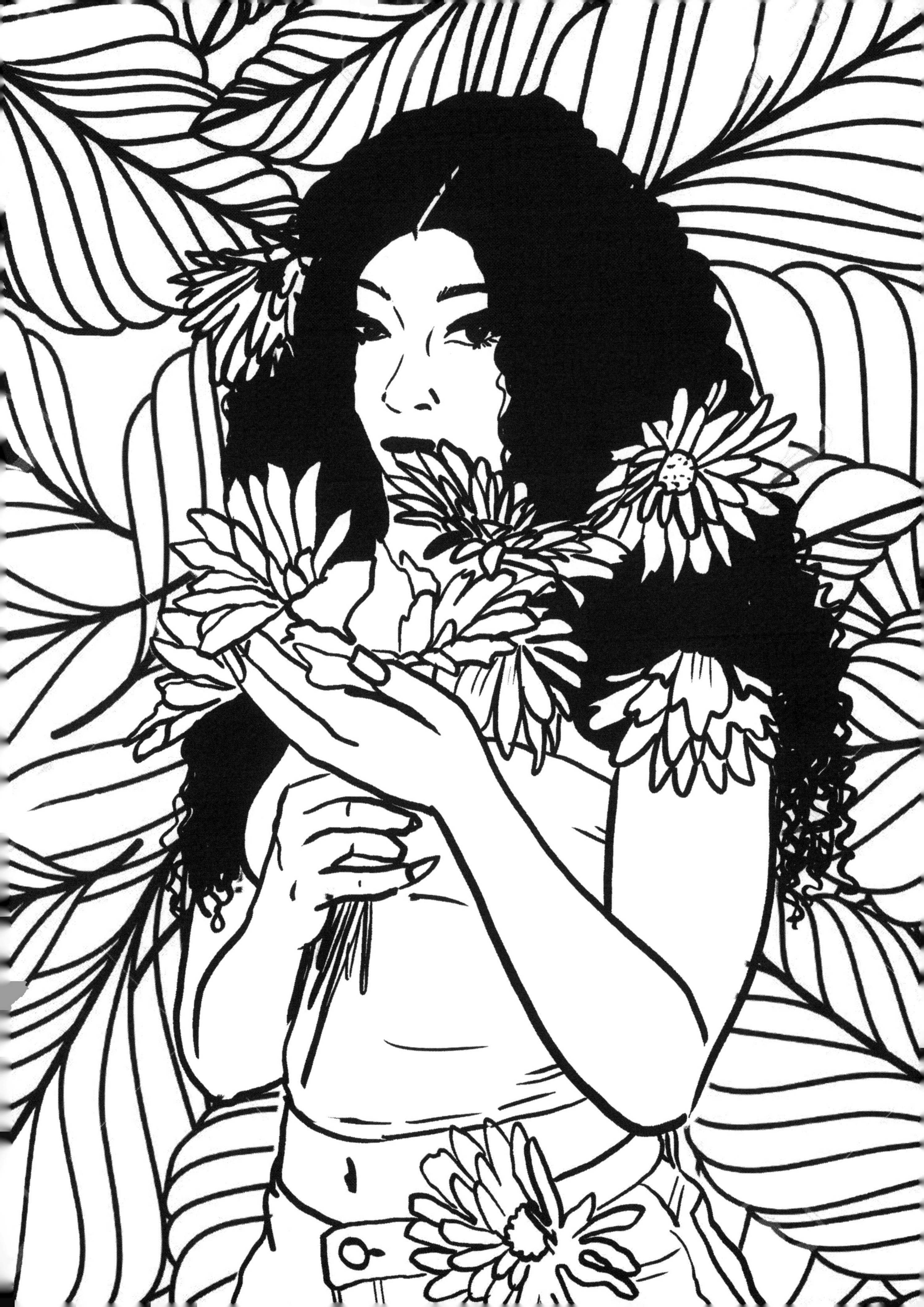

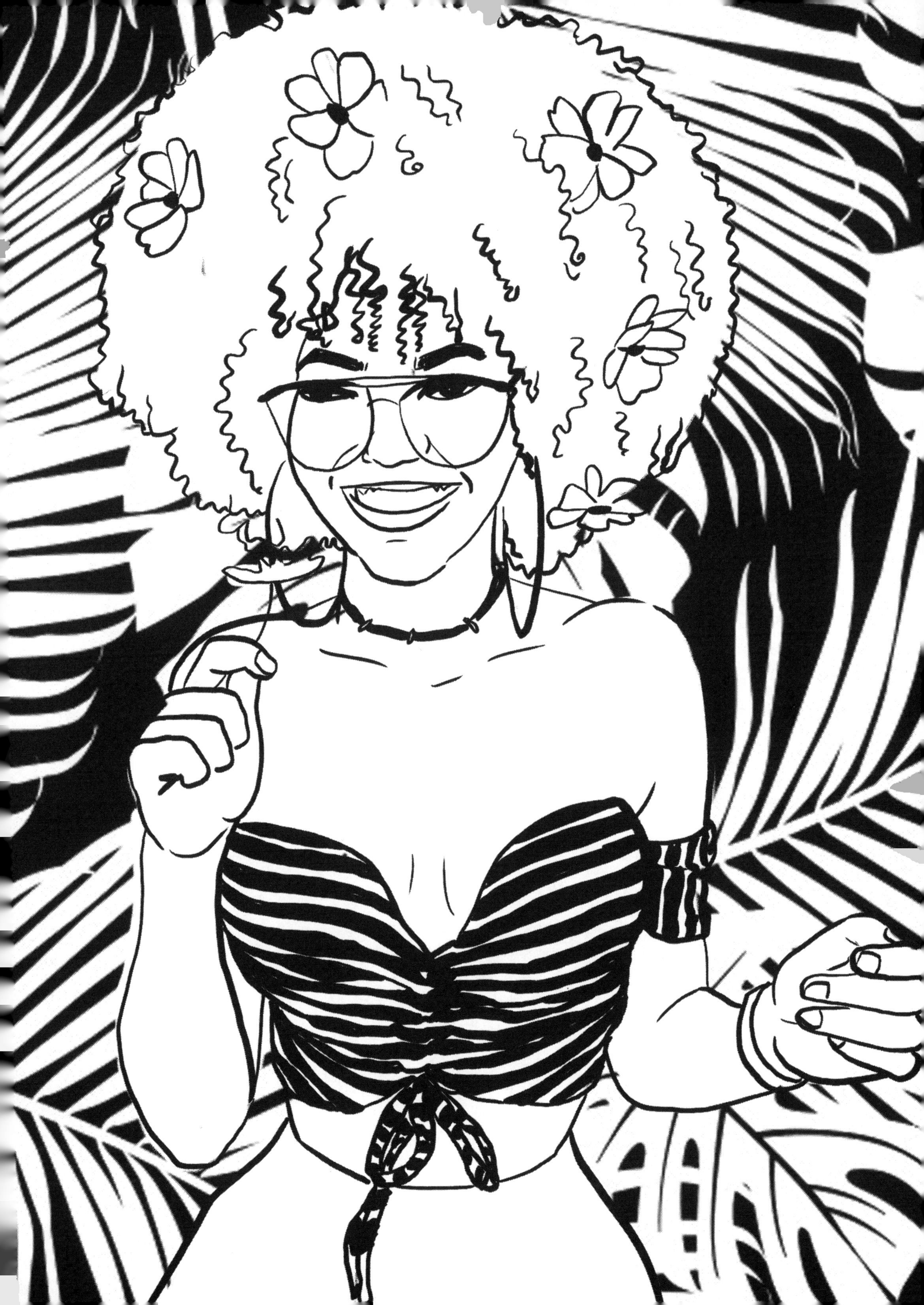

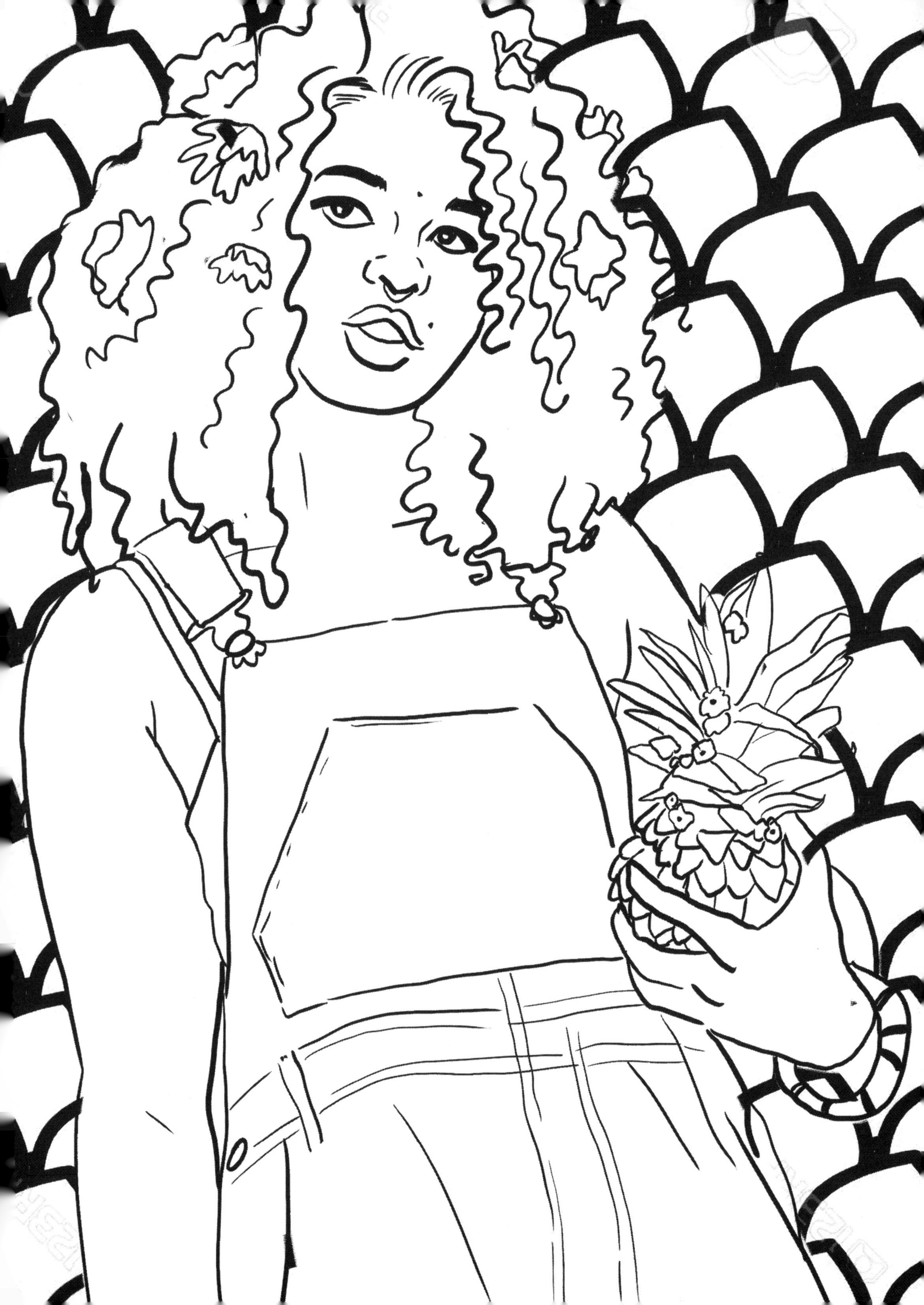

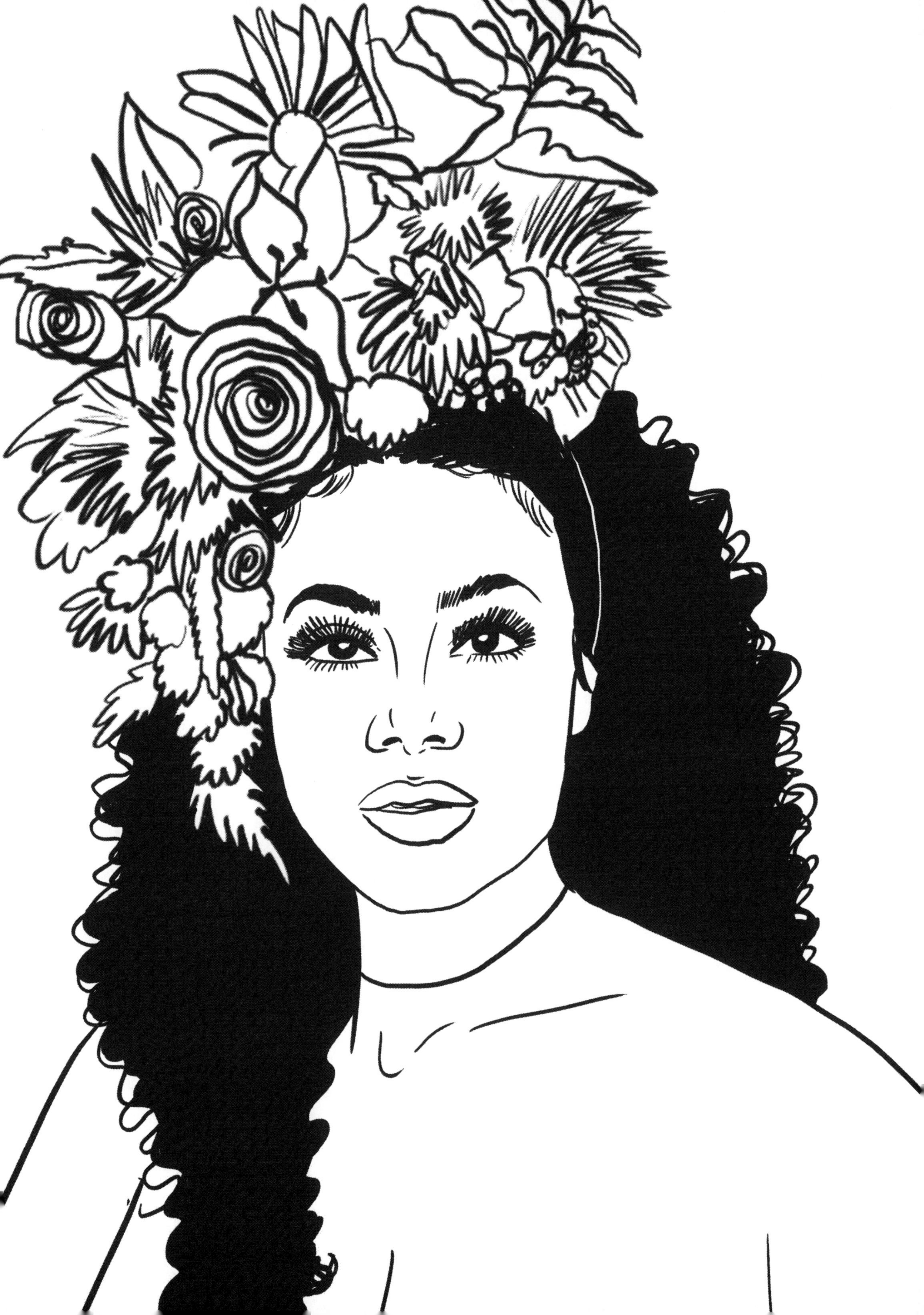

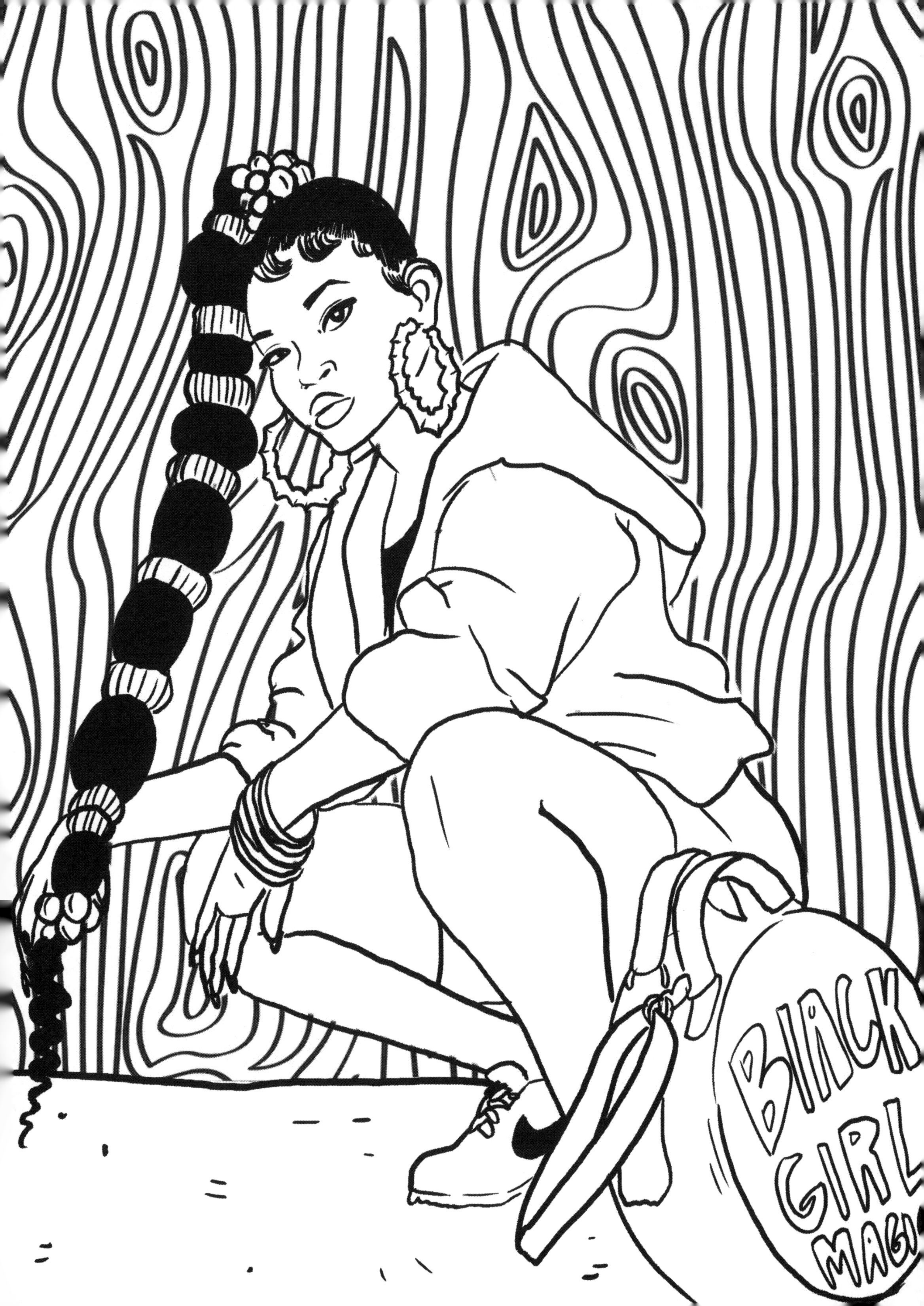
BLACK GIRL MAGI

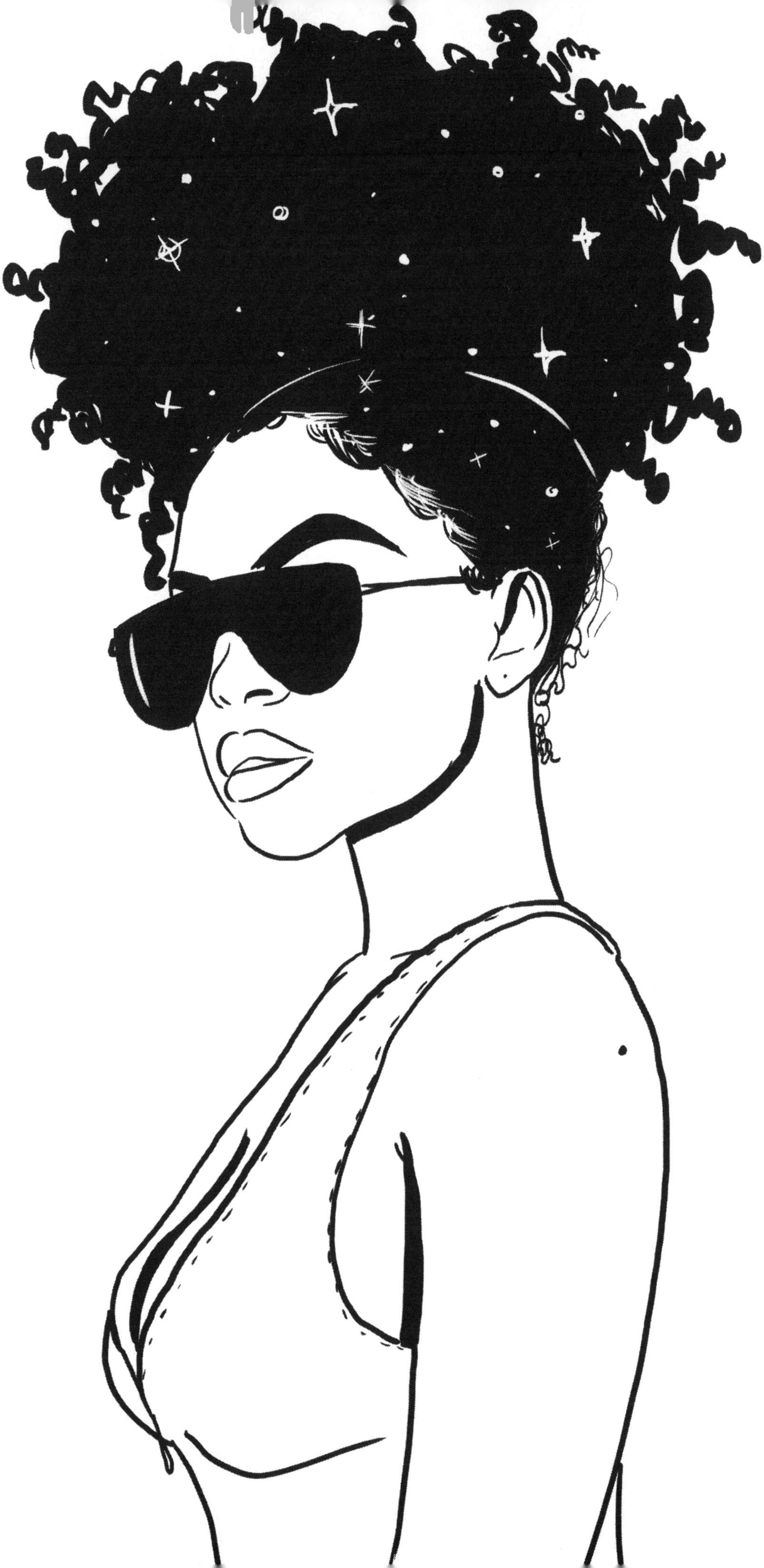

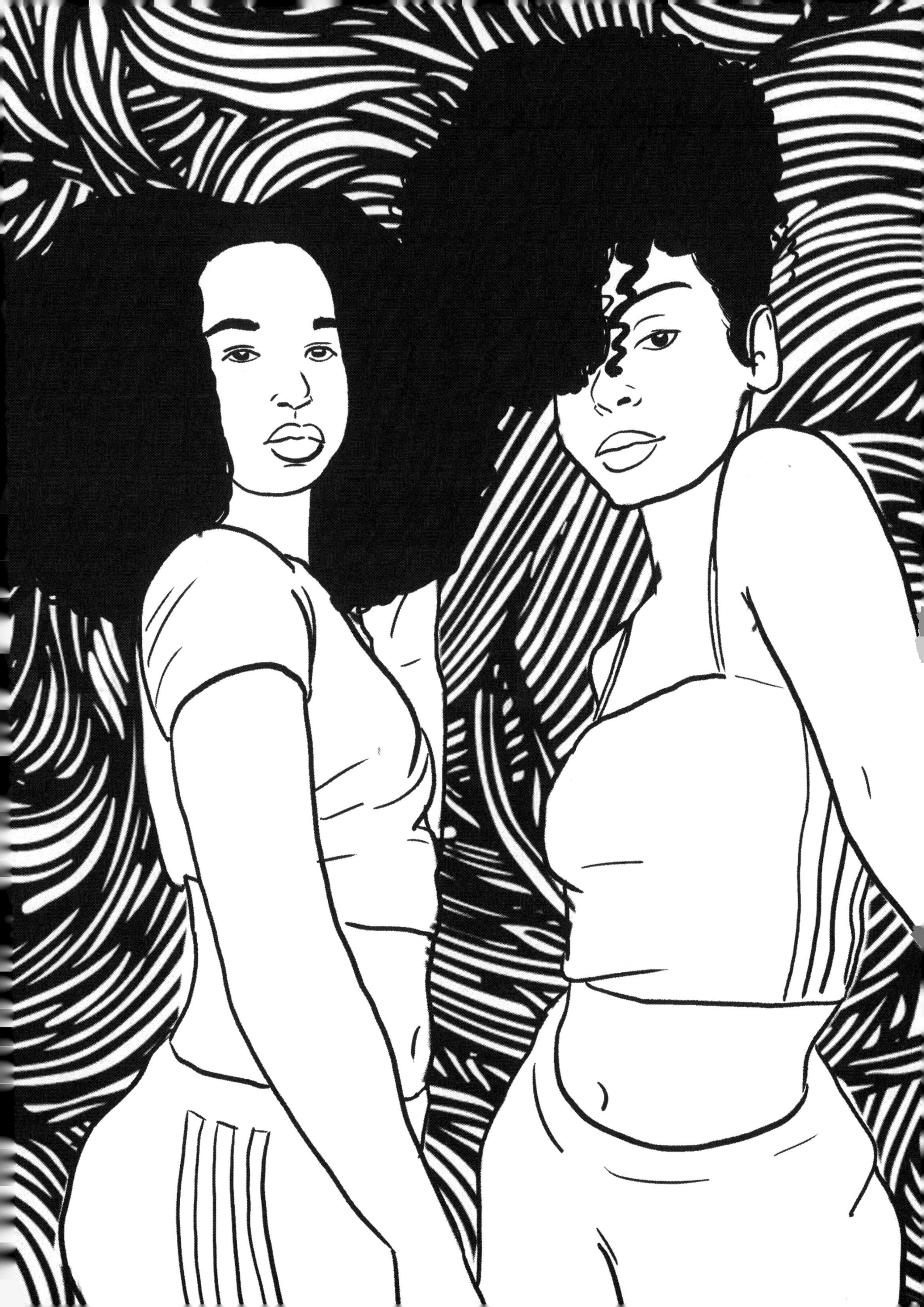

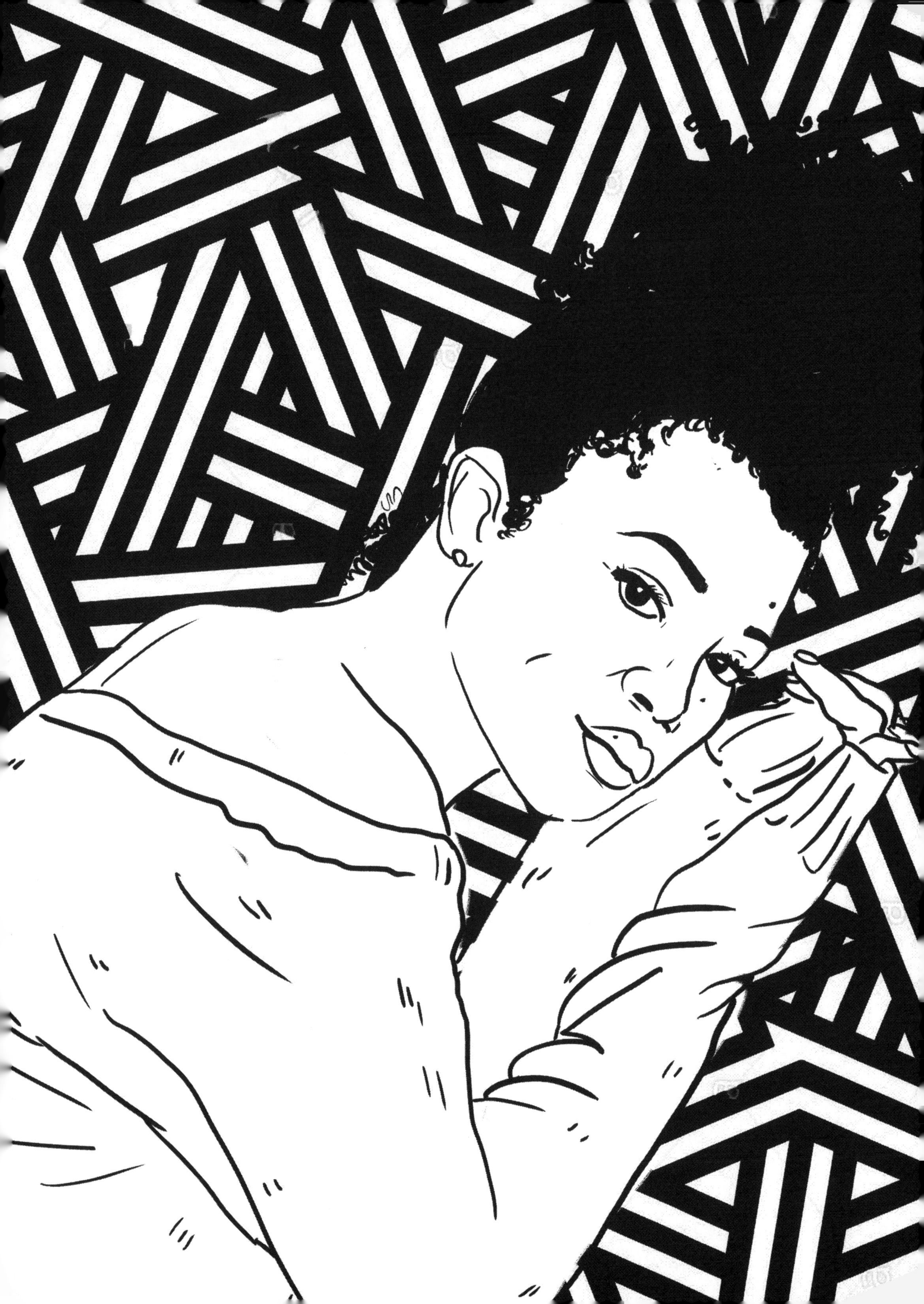

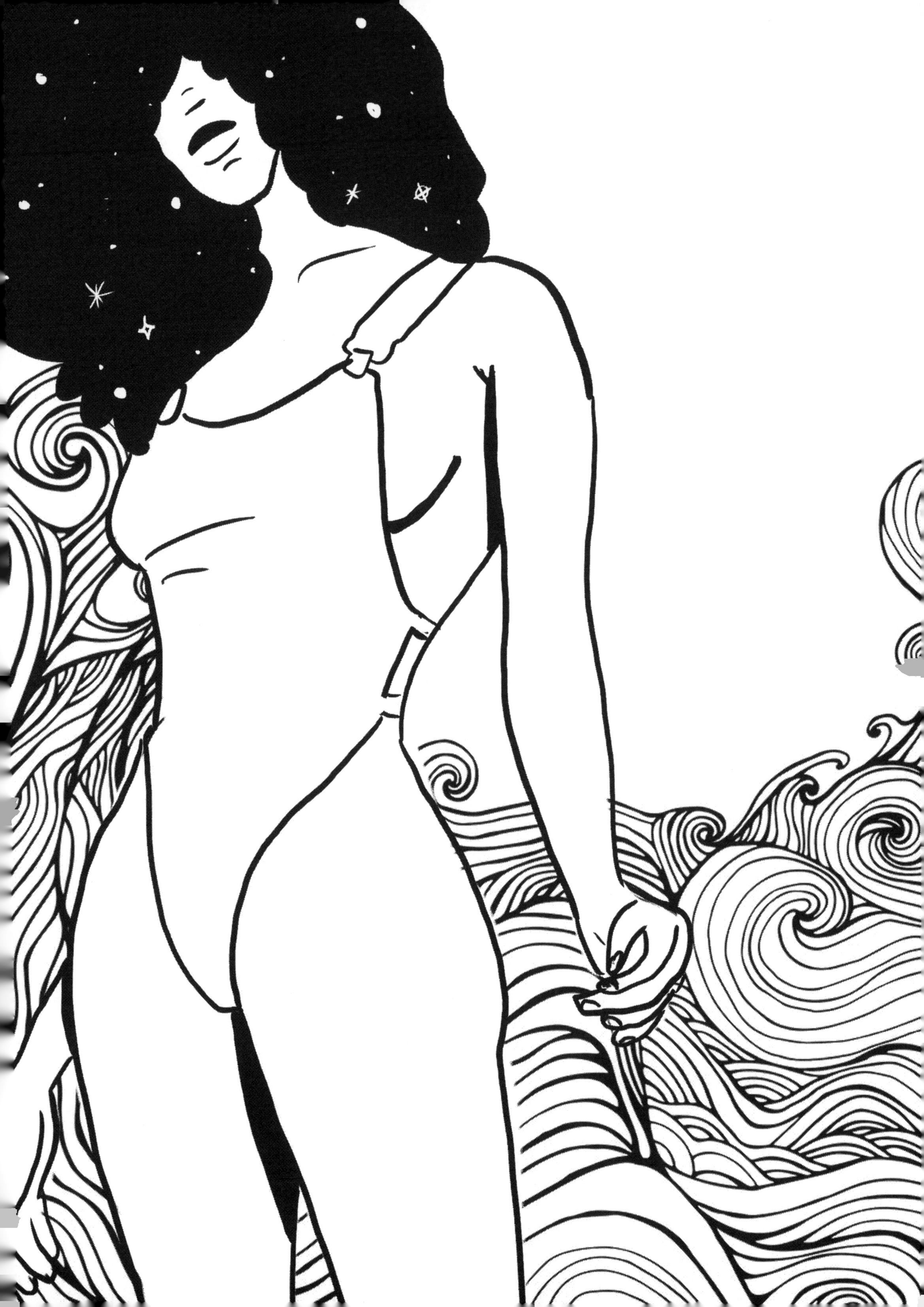

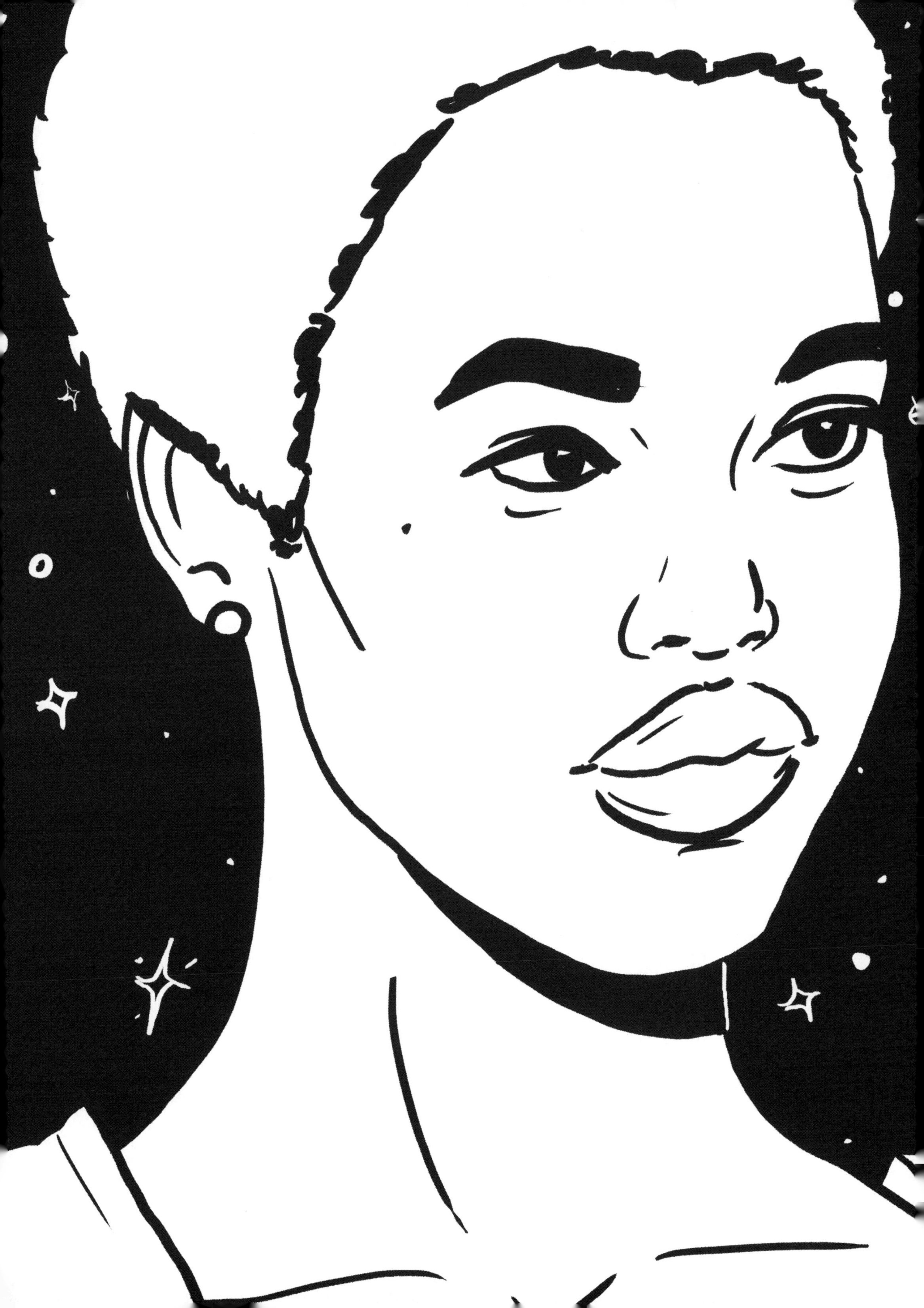

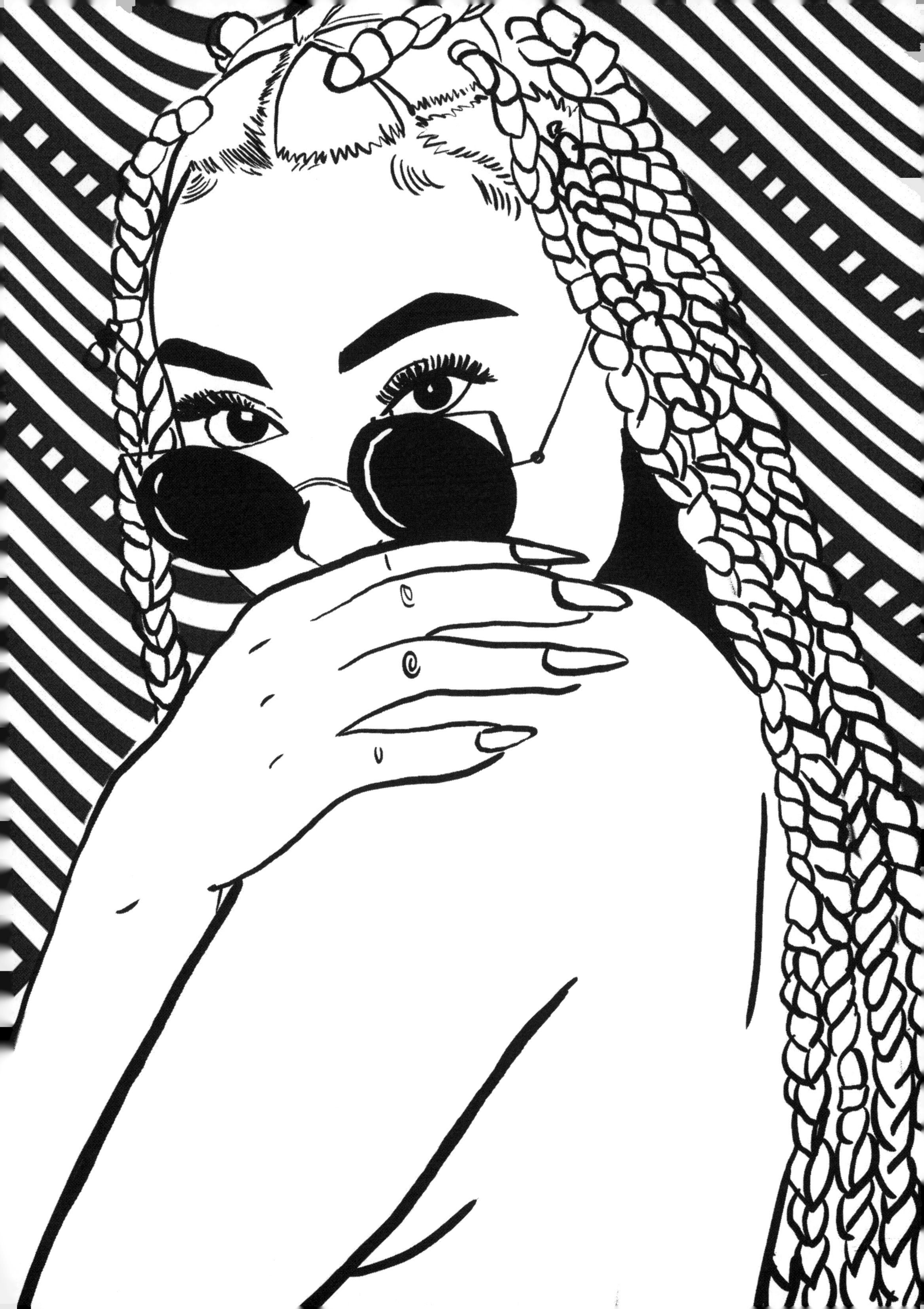

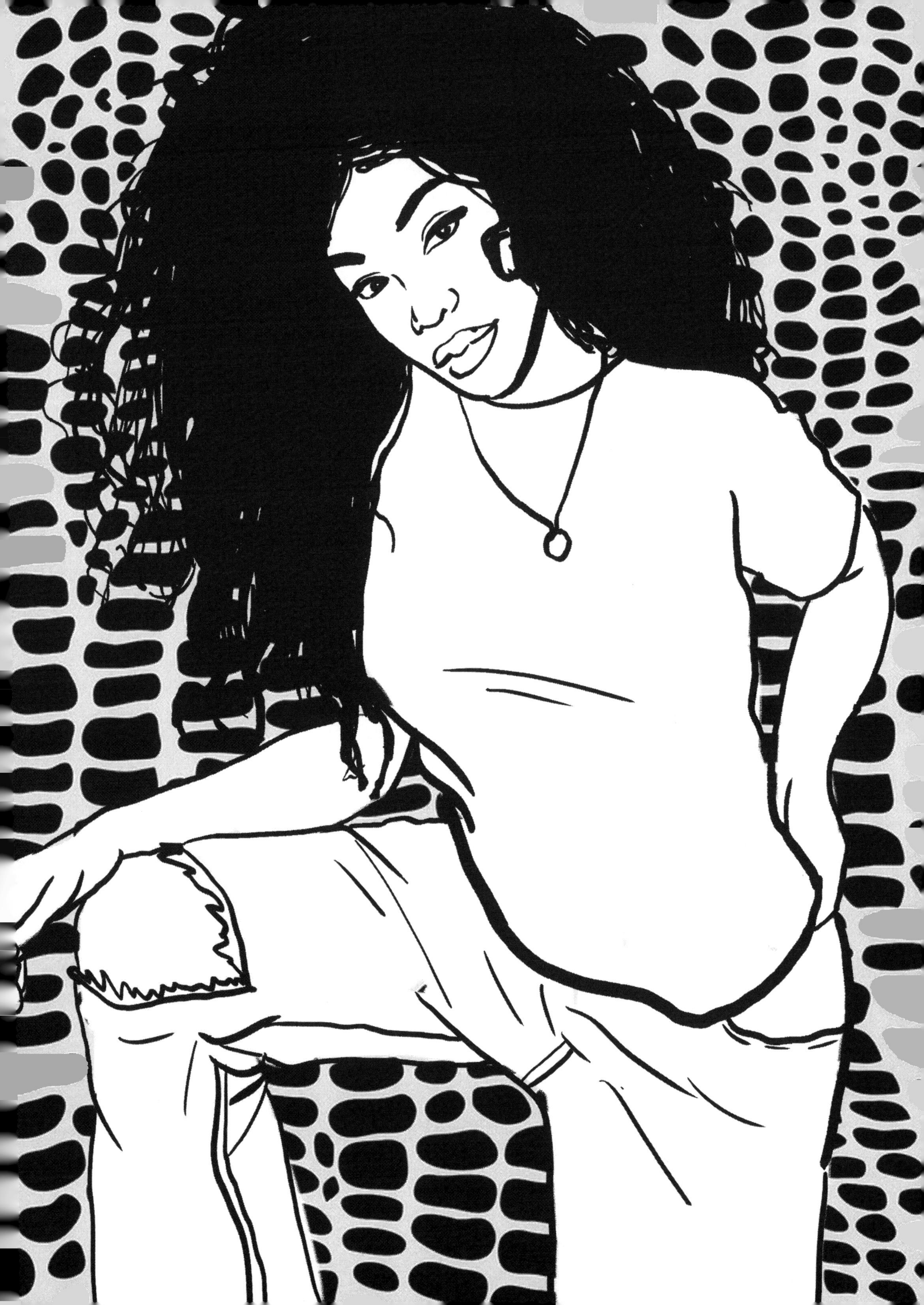

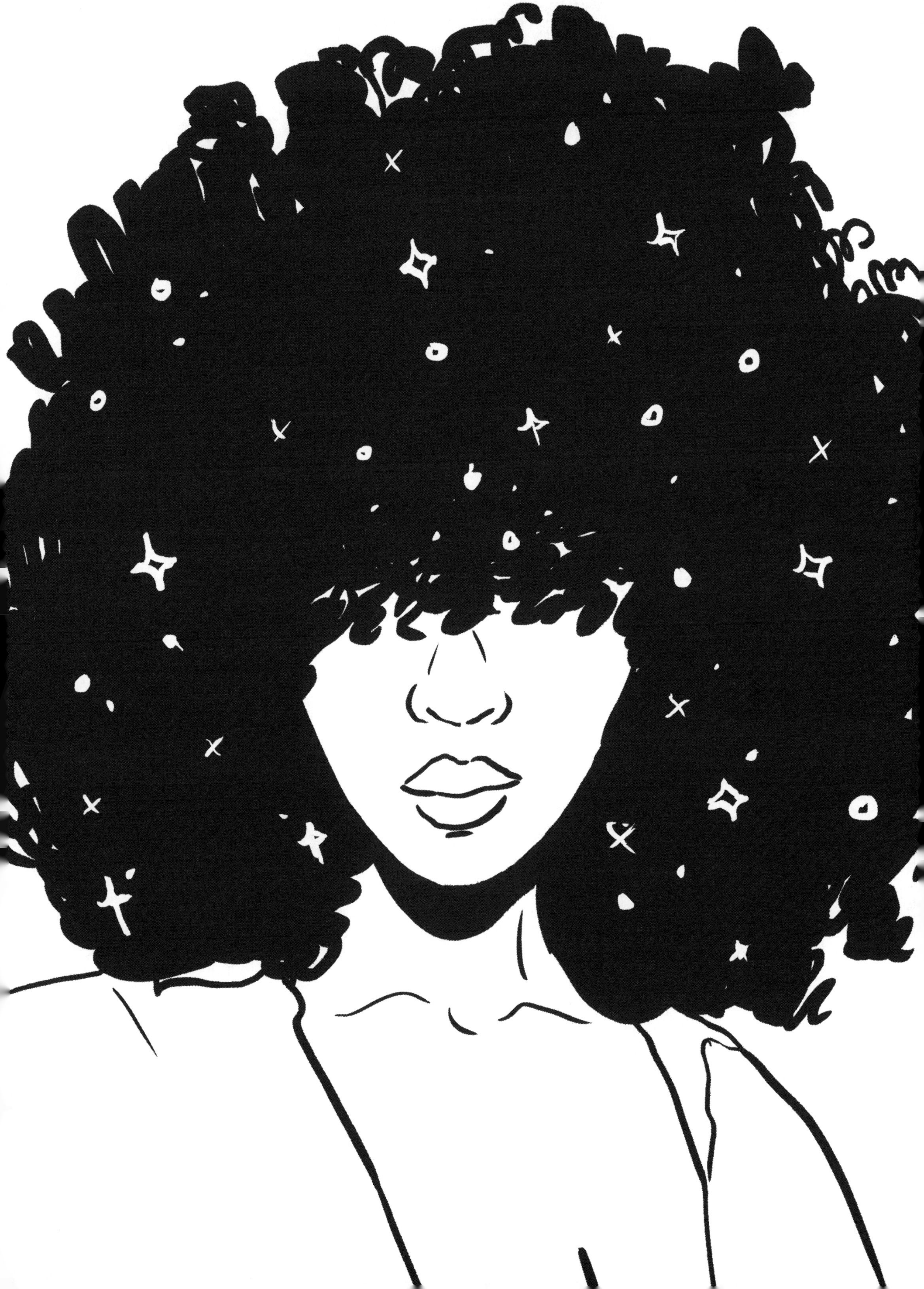

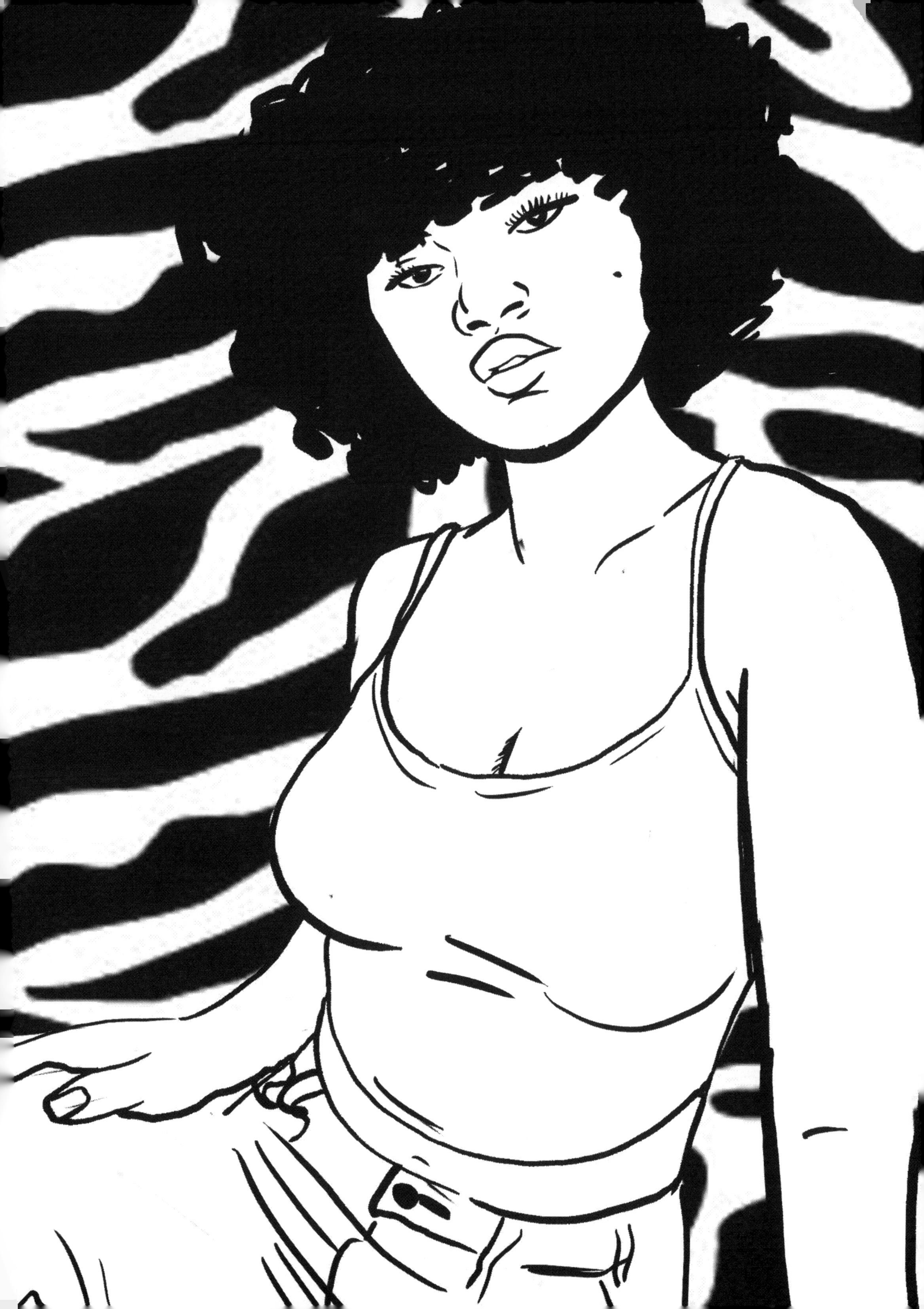

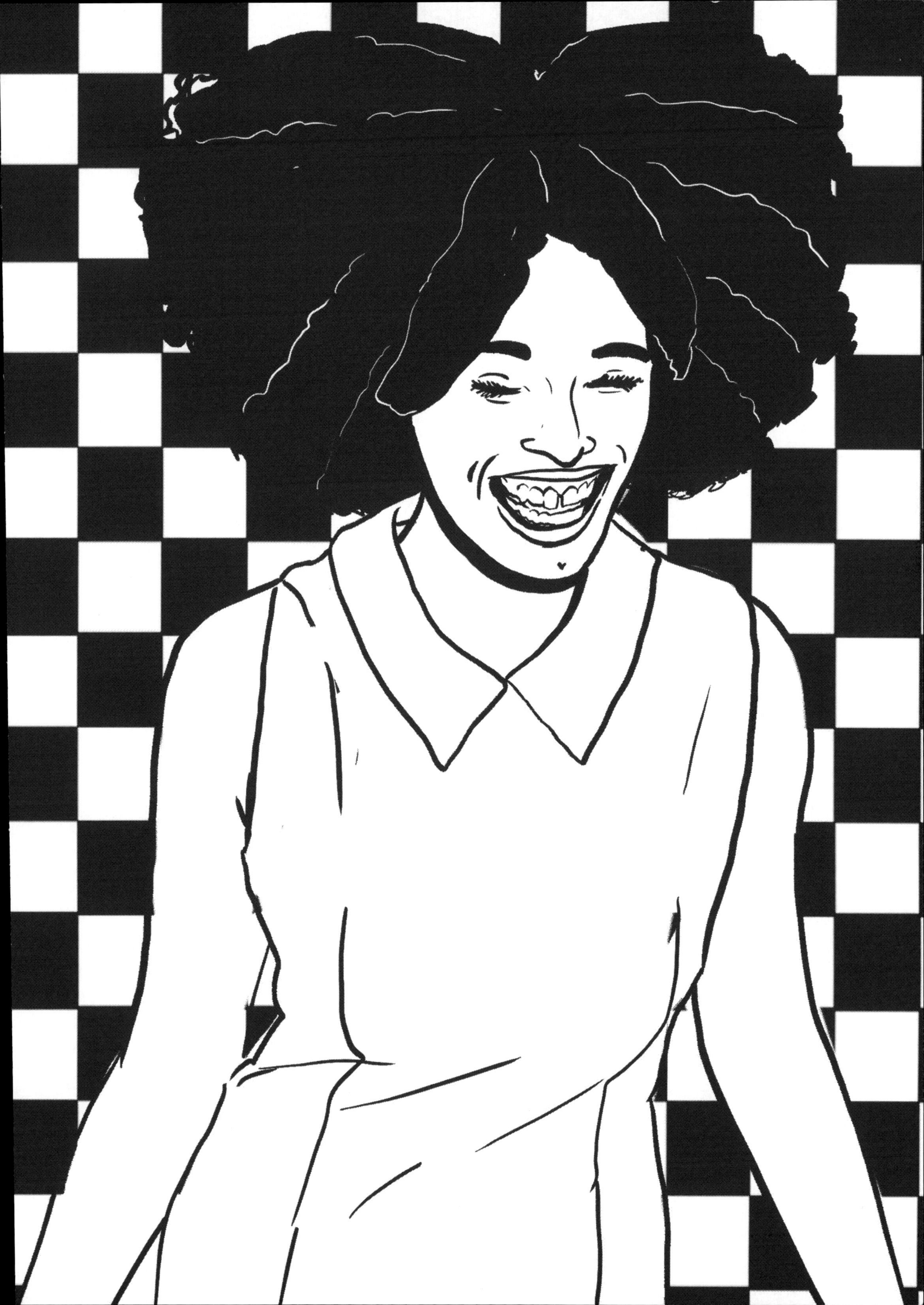

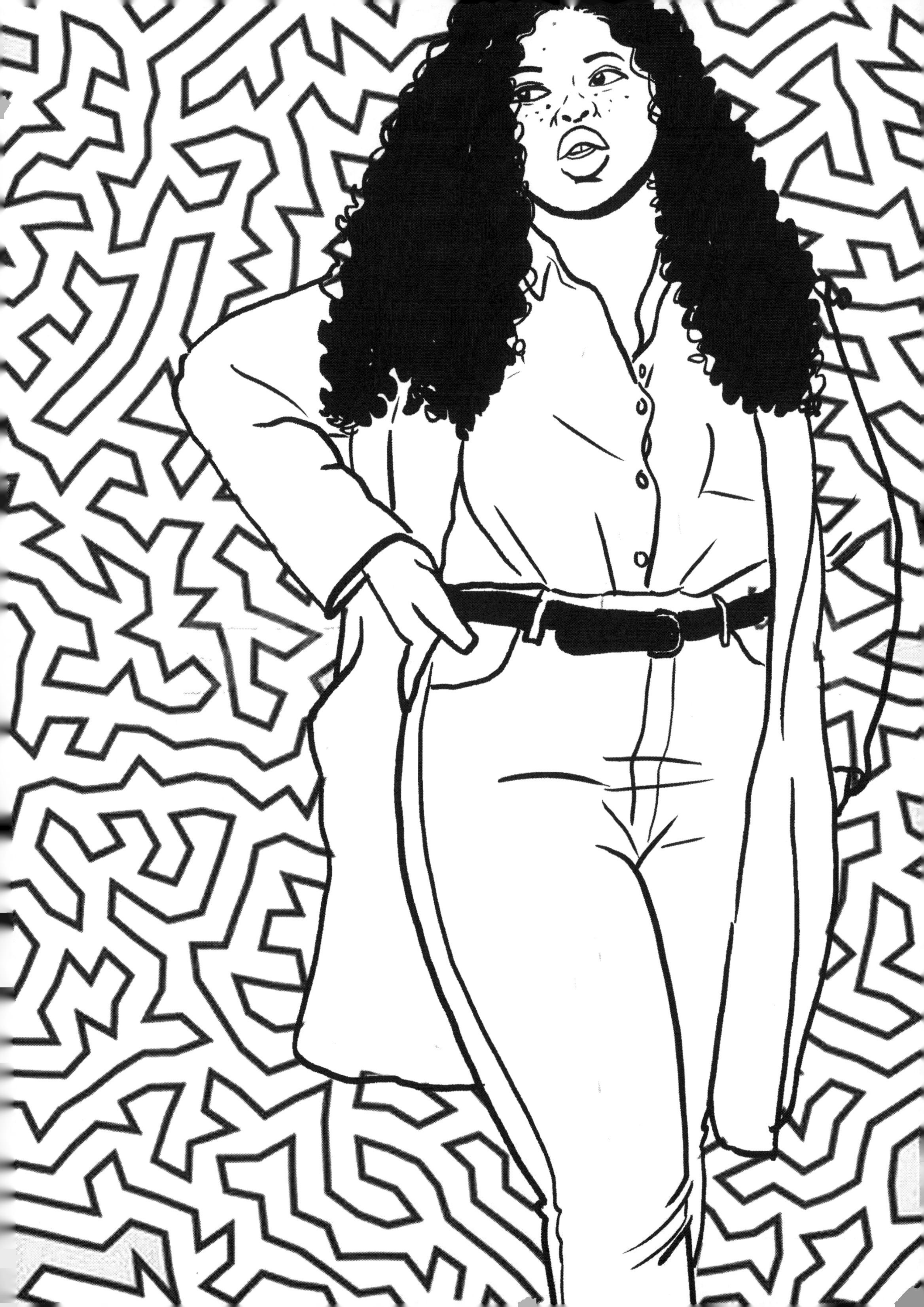

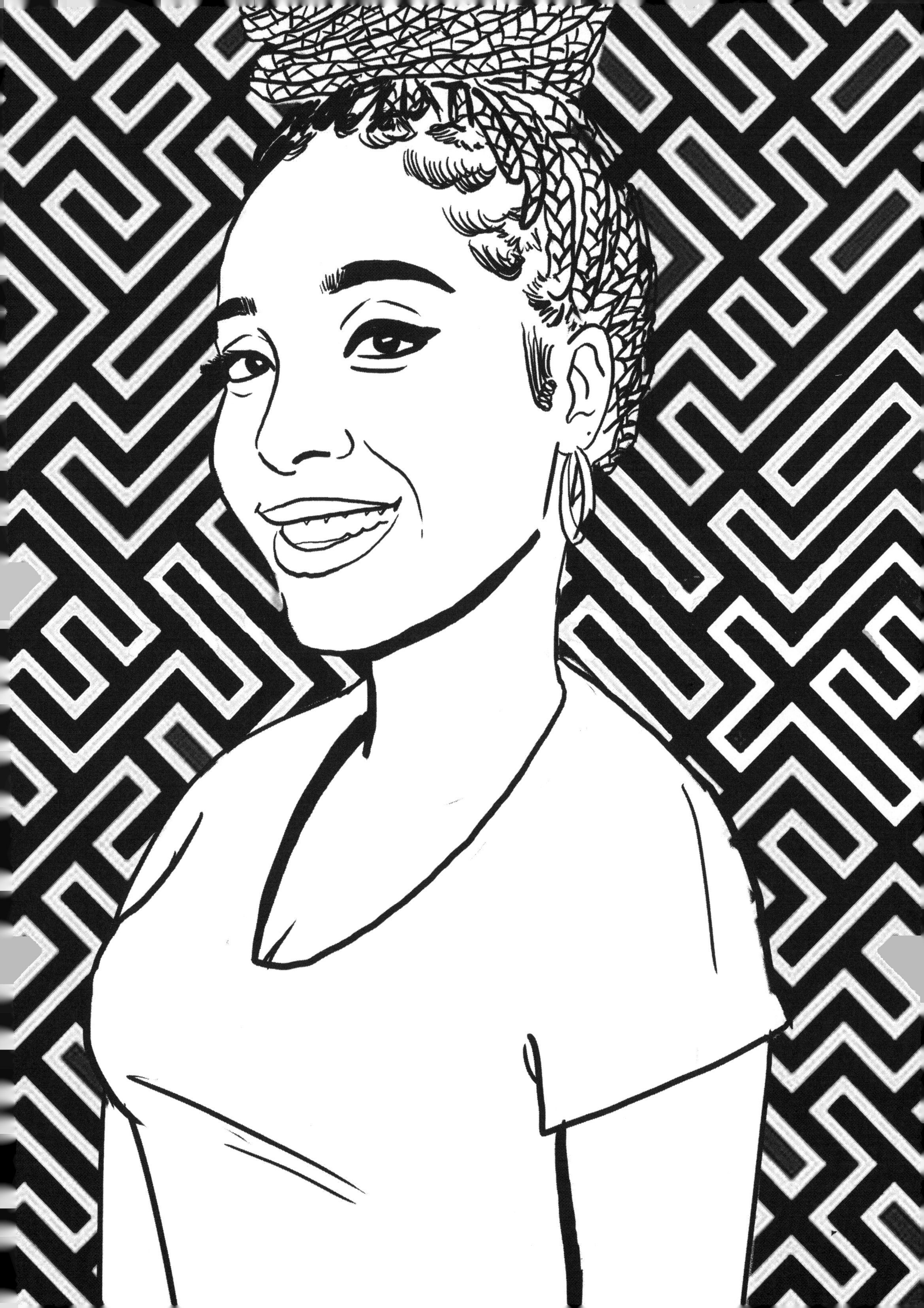

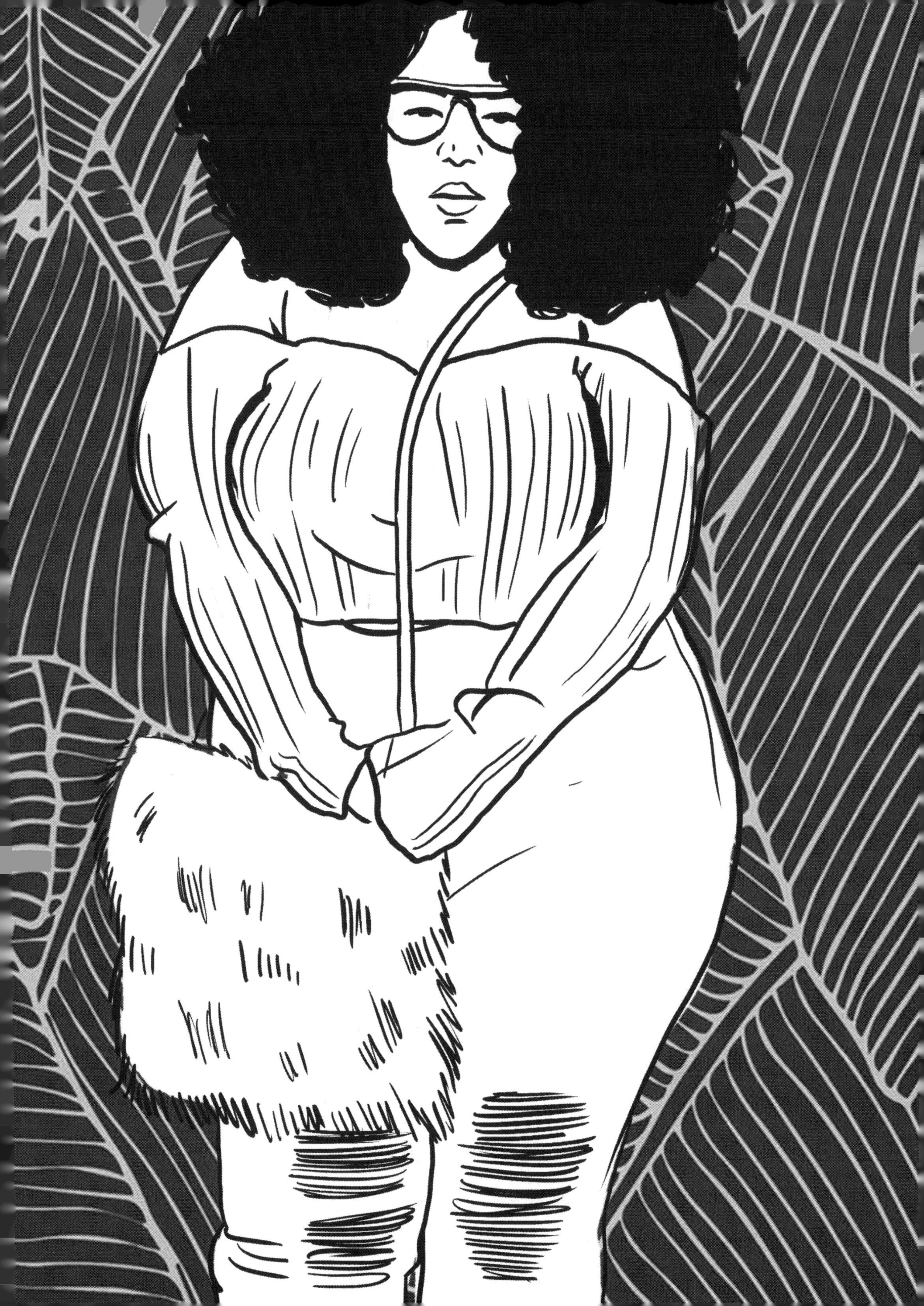

Made in the USA
Columbia, SC
07 February 2020

87618574R00043